JOURNEYS

Write-In Reader

Grade 2

Be a Reading Detective!

A detective looks for clues. You can look for clues, too. You can be a Reading Detective.

When you read, think about these questions:

▶ **Who?**

▶ **Where?**

▶ **When?**

▶ **What?**

▶ **Why?**

Look for clues to help you answer the questions.

"Let's try it! Follow the trail..."

Try It !

Read the story. Think about these questions:

Who?   **Where?**   **When?**

Marco and Papa are at the beach. It is sunny and hot. Papa hums a tune.

"This is a great birthday!" Marco says.

"Look, Marco!" Papa says. "Look at that!"

Answer the questions.

1. Who is the story about?

2. Where does the story take place?

3. When does the story take place?

Can you find clues to help you? If you can, you are a Reading Detective!

Contents

✓ **TARGET VOCABULARY**

curly

row

stood

straight

My Friends

1 My friend Lisa has **straight** hair. It is very smooth.

Tell about a friend who has straight hair.

_____

_____

_____

2 My friend Miguel has curls and waves in his hair. He has **curly** hair.

Name a friend who has <u>curly</u> hair.

_____

3 Paquita is my friend. We played hide-and-seek. Paquita hid behind a bush. It **stood** six feet tall!

Tell about someone who <u>stood</u> taller than you.

_____

_____

_____

4 Bart and his friends played leap frog. They lined up in a **row**. Then they took turns and jumped.

In what other game can kids line up in a <u>row</u>?

_____

_____

_____

Best ♥♥ Friends

by Margaret Maugenest

Mai and Jenny were best friends. They lived next door to each other.

A tree **stood** between their homes. It had a **straight** trunk. The top of the tree looked like **curly** green hair.

Stop   Think   Write

VOCABULARY

The treetop looks a lot like

_____ green hair.

4

Jenny and Mai wrote notes to each other. They put the notes in a tree. It was their secret hiding place.

It was Jenny's birthday. Mai got Jenny a present. She wrote Jenny a note.

Stop **Think** **Write**

CAUSE AND EFFECT

Mai gets Jenny a present for her

_____ .

The note said to come to Mai's house. Mai put a red bow around the note. She put it in the tree. Then she waited.

Jenny did not come. Mai checked the tree. Her note was gone.

SEQUENCE OF EVENTS

Stop **Think** **Write**

Mai puts the note in the tree. What does she do after that?

_____

_____

Mai looked at Jenny's house. She saw kids. They lined up in a **row**. They had presents. They went into Jenny's house.

Jenny was having a birthday party! Why didn't she invite Mai?

Stop **Think** **Write**

VOCABULARY

Who lined up in a <u>row</u>?

_____

_____

_____

7

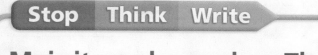

Mai sat on her swing. She felt mad. Jenny came. "Why aren't you at my party?" she said.

Mai got off the swing. She stood tall. "You didn't invite me!" she said.

Mai sits on her swing. Then

_____ **comes.**

"I DID invite you. I put a note in the tree," said Jenny.

The girls heard a noise. They looked up. They saw a bird in a nest. The nest had paper. It had a red bow.

Stop **Think** **Write**

SEQUENCE OF EVENTS

Jenny and Mai hear a noise and look up. They

see a _____ in a nest.

"That bird took our notes. It took the ribbon. It used them for its nest!" said Mai.

Jenny and Mai still write notes to each other. Now they put their notes in a box. They are still best friends.

Stop | Think | Write

MAIN IDEAS AND DETAILS

The bird used the notes and ribbon to make its

_____ .

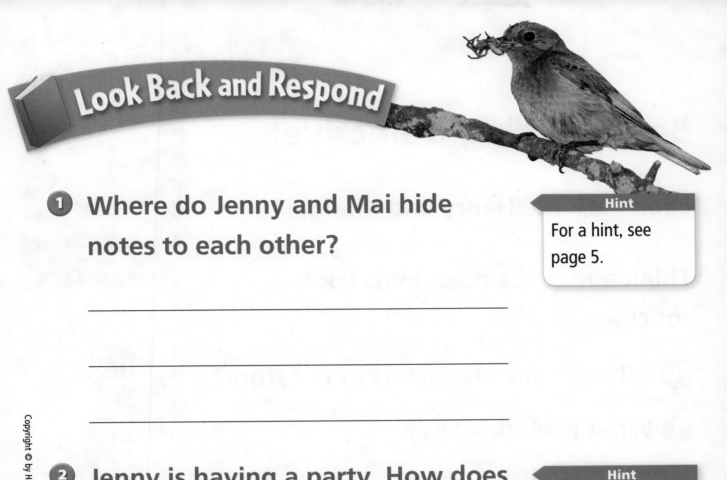

Look Back and Respond

1 Where do Jenny and Mai hide notes to each other?

Hint
For a hint, see page 5.

_____

_____

_____

2 Jenny is having a party. How does Mai feel?

Hint
For a hint, see page 8.

_____

_____

_____

3 The girls see the nest. After that, where do they put notes?

Hint
For a hint, see page 10.

_____

_____

_____

Be a Reading Detective!

Look back at "Henry and Mudge."

Think about the questions. Look for clues.

"Henry and Mudge"
Student Book pp. 15–25

1 **Who** are the characters in the story?

2 **What** is Mudge like?

11A

Write your answer.

1 **Who** are the characters in the story?

_____

_____

_____

_____

_____

Talk about question 2. Tell about the clues you found.

2 **What** is Mudge like?

11B

Family Parties

Check the answer.

1 Grandma and Grandpa _____ us each summer. They stay at our house. We have a big party for them.

☐ **drooled**   ☐ **visit**   ☐ **stood**

2 It is my birthday! We have a party.

Dad puts a _____ on my head.

☐ **crown**   ☐ **row**   ☐ **cousin**

12

3 My _____ Kaya had a baby. We gave a party. People brought gifts for the baby.

☐ **crown**   ☐ **piano**   ☐ **cousin**

4 Have you ever <u>remembered</u> a very special party? What made it special?

_____

_____

_____

5 Who would you like to <u>visit</u>? Why?

_____

_____

_____

The Nicest Party

by Maria Sánchez

I am so happy. Uncle Takada and Aunt Onida are coming to **visit**. Their daughter, Tala, is coming, too.

I have not met Tala. I've seen pictures. I like looking at family pictures.

> ### Stop Think Write
>
> VOCABULARY
>
> Uncle Takada, Aunt Onida, and Tala are coming
>
> to _____.

14

"We must have a family party!" said Mother.

"May I help?" I asked.

"Yes, Nita," said Mother. "We must shop for party things."

Stop   Think   Write

MAIN IDEAS AND DETAILS

What will Nita and her mother buy?

_____

_____

_____

We went to the party store.
We got things for the table.
I **remembered** to get balloons.
We got a **crown** for Tala.

"I can't wait for the party!"
I said.

Stop | **Think** | **Write**

UNDERSTANDING CHARACTERS

How does Nita feel?

16

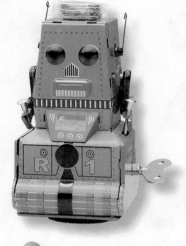

"We have more shopping to do," said Mother.

We went to the toy store. I saw a stuffed bear. We got it for my **cousin** Tala.

Stop | Think | Write

The bear is for Nita's _____ Tala.

17

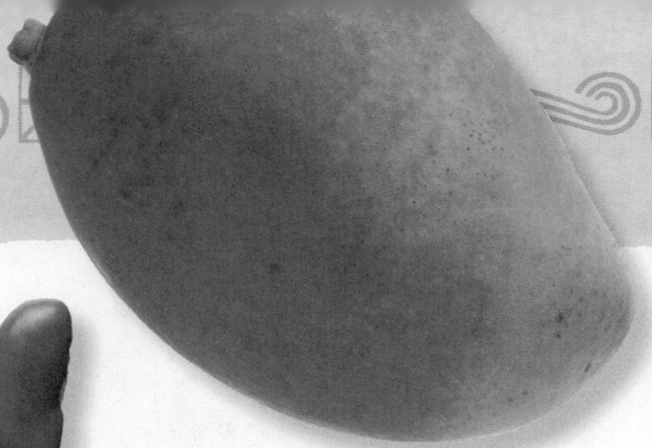

We went to the market next. We got fruit. We got vegetables. We got other good things to eat.

We put the food in our cart. Soon we had all we needed.

CAUSE AND EFFECT

Why do Mother and Nita go to the market?

_____

_____

_____

Then we went home.
Mother cooked. I helped.
"It smells so good!" I said.
We put out the party
things. "Now we are
ready!" said Mother.

Stop **Think** **Write**

SEQUENCE OF EVENTS

Mother and Nita cook. Then they are

_____ for the party.

It was party time! Everyone in our family came. We ate. We laughed. My aunt played music. Tala wore her crown.

"This is a special party!" said Uncle Takada. "Thank you!"

Stop | Think | Write

COMPARE AND CONTRAST

How are the people at the party alike?

_____

_____

_____

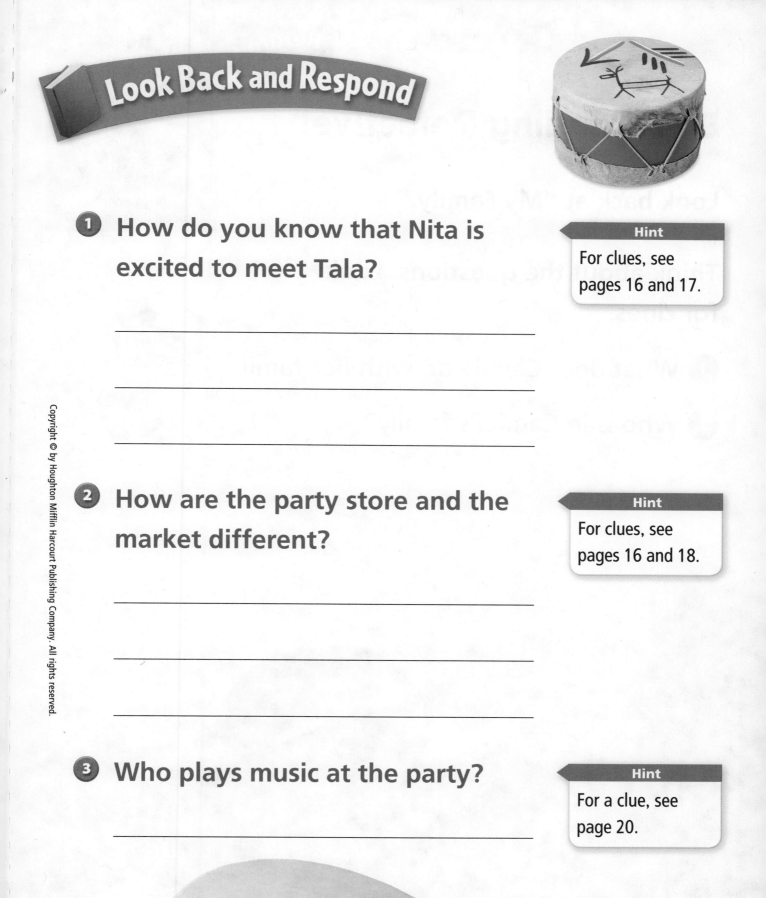

Look Back and Respond

1 How do you know that Nita is excited to meet Tala?

_____

_____

_____

Hint
For clues, see pages 16 and 17.

2 How are the party store and the market different?

_____

_____

_____

Hint
For clues, see pages 16 and 18.

3 Who plays music at the party?

_____

Hint
For a clue, see page 20.

Return to

"My Family"
Student Book pp. 43–57

Be a Reading Detective!

Look back at "My Family."

Think about the questions. Look for clues.

1 **What** does Camila do with her family?

2 **Who** is in Camila's family?

Write your answer.

1 **What** does Camila do with her family?

_____

_____

_____

_____

_____

Talk about question 2. Tell about the clues you found.

2 **Who** is in Camila's family?

✓ TARGET VOCABULARY

coat

hairy

litter

mammals

Animals in the House!

Check the answer.

1 A dog's _____ can be brown, white, or other colors.
   ☐ **coat** ☐ **walk** ☐ **bark**

2 My cat gave birth to a _____ of four kittens.
   ☐ **coat** ☐ **pile** ☐ **litter**

3 <u>Mammals</u> feed their young milk.
Give an example of a pet mammal.

_____

_____

_____

4 Why is a <u>hairy</u> pet more work than
a pet with short hair?

_____

_____

_____

5 How can you keep your pet's <u>coat</u>
shiny and smooth?

_____

_____

_____

The Best Pet

by Judy Rosenbaum

Are you looking for a pet?
A dog is a fine pet. A dog
will play with you. It
can be a pal.

You can find a good
dog at a pet shelter.
Or a mother dog in
your neighborhood
may have a **litter**
of pups.

Stop **Think** **Write**

Does the word <u>litter</u> name one animal or a
group of animals? What clue does the sentence
give you?

_____

_____

A dog can be a big job, though. You have to walk it. You must brush its **coat**. A dog can eat a lot, too.

Dogs won't always do the right thing. Some dogs chew everything. Dogs can be loud. Some dogs like to run off.

Are you sure about a dog?

Stop	Think	Write

MAIN IDEA AND DETAIILS

Give one detail that tells why having a dog can be a big job.

_____

_____

25

You could get a cat. Cats are fine pets. They love to jump, climb, and play.

A cat can be a big job, though. You must brush its fur. You must feed it. You don't have to walk a cat, but you need to spend time with it.

AUTHOR'S PURPOSE

Why does the author give both good and bad points about having a pet cat?

_____

_____

Cats won't always do the right thing.
Some cats scratch tables and chairs.
Some cats hide and spring out at you.
Many cats like to be up at night. So they
might make noise while you are trying
to sleep.

Are you sure about a cat?

Stop **Think** **Write**

AUTHOR'S PURPOSE

Why do you think the author uses the words some and many when telling about cats?

_____

_____

27

What if you want a quiet pet? Then don't look just at **mammals**. Think about fish!

Fish make no noise at all. They don't even whisper. They don't get out of the house and run off. They stay in their tank. They don't scratch things. They don't even have paws!

Stop　Think　Write

VOCABULARY

What <u>mammals</u> has the author talked about in this selection?

_____

_____

Fish are not **hairy** like dogs or cats. So you don't have to brush them. They eat only a little bit. They don't need to be walked. You don't need any fish leashes! Fish are easy to care for. You just have to clean the tank.

Stop Think Write

AUTHOR'S PURPOSE

What is the author's main purpose in writing about fish?

_____

_____

29

But...

If you want a pet to run around with, you need to look for something else.

MAKE INFERENCES

What kind of person might choose to have a dog or cat instead of a fish?

_____

_____

1 Fish do not have a

_____ coat.

Hint

For a clue, look on page 29.

2 What is one reason that dogs are more work than cats?

_____

_____

_____

Hint

Look on pages 25 and 26.

3 Did the author write "The Best Pet" mainly to entertain readers or mainly to give information? How can you tell?

_____

_____

_____

Hint

There are clues on almost every page!

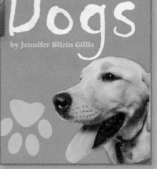

Return to

Dogs
by Jennifer Blizin Gillis

"Dogs"
Student Book pp. 75–89

Be a Reading Detective!

Look back at "Dogs."

Think about the questions.
Look for clues.

1 **Who** can take care of a dog?

2 **What** does a dog need?

Write your answer.

1 **Who** can take care of a dog?

_____

_____

_____

_____

_____

Talk about question 2. Tell about the clues you found.

2 **What** does a dog need?

breeze

dangerous

scare

screaming

Different Kinds of Places

1 A **dangerous** place isn't right for you. A street is dangerous. It isn't safe. You might get hurt.

Name a <u>dangerous</u> place.

_____

_____

2 Some places might **scare** you. No one likes to be afraid. Scary places are not right for you!

Name two places that might <u>scare</u> a cat.

_____

_____

3 Noisy places aren't much fun. People might be **screaming**. It's hard to like a noisy place.

Name a noisy place where people might be <u>screaming</u>.

_____

_____

4 Is a quiet place right for you? Do you like to hear the birds sing? Do you like to hear the **breeze** blow?

Name a place where you might hear the <u>breeze</u>.

_____

_____

Diva the Dancer

by Duncan Searl

Diva was a dog. She was also a dancer. Diva needed a job.

"Maybe I can work at the circus," Diva said.

Diva went to the circus. She asked for a job dancing.

Stop | Think | Write

CAUSE AND EFFECT

Diva went to the circus to get a

_____.

34

The circus people had only one kind of job. "Work up here with us," they said.

Diva shook her head. "Those jobs look **dangerous**! I just want to dance."

Stop | Think | Write

The circus job looked _____ to Diva.

Diva went to Officer Lee for a job.
"You can help me catch bad guys," said
Officer Lee.

"No, thanks," said Diva. "That might
scare me. Besides, I want to dance."

Stop   Think   Write

VOCABULARY

What kind of people <u>scare</u> Diva?

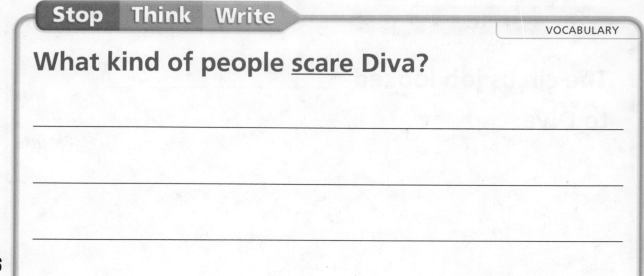

Mr. Ray wanted a nice quiet pet. Diva got the job. Diva was happy. She began to dance.

"No dancing!" Mr. Ray said. "I want peace and quiet!" So Diva moved on.

Stop **Think** **Write**

CAUSE AND EFFECT

Diva left Mr. Ray because she could not

_____ **there.**

37

Mrs. Bibb wanted a dog for her boys. "I'm great with children," Diva told her.

The Bibb boys weren't great for Diva. They were always **screaming**. There was too much noise for Diva to dance.

Stop **Think** **Write**

VOCABULARY

The Bibb boys made noise by

_____ .

Diva left the Bibbs. Outside, she heard music in the **breeze**.

Diva followed the music. She came to a house. It was near a park.

Stop Think Write

STORY STRUCTURE

The music came from a _____ .

The house was a dance school.

"I need a helper," the teacher told Diva.
"Can you dance?"

Diva began to dance. And she's been
dancing ever since.

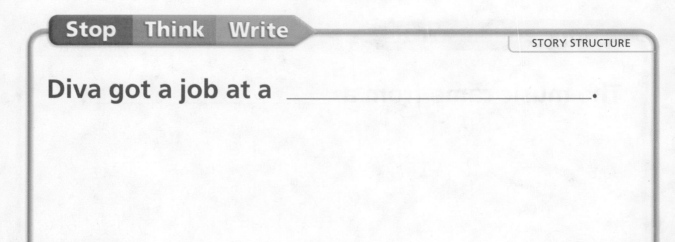

Stop | Think | Write

STORY STRUCTURE

Diva got a job at a _____.

Look Back and Respond

1 Why did Diva go to the circus?

_____

_____

_____

Hint

For a clue, see page 34.

2 Why did Diva leave the Bibbs?

_____

_____

_____

Hint

For a clue, see page 38.

3 Did Diva get the right job in the end? How do you know?

_____

_____

_____

Hint

For a clue, see page 40.

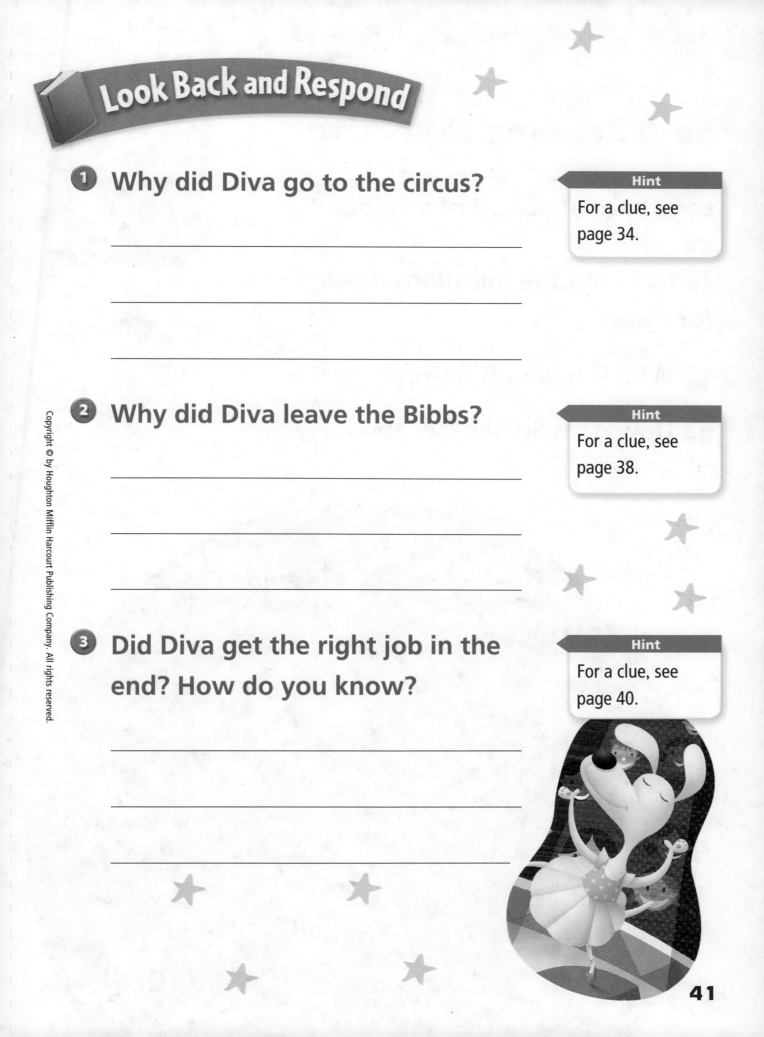

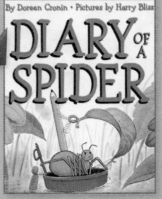

Return to

By Doreen Cronin • Pictures by Harry Bliss

DIARY OF A SPIDER

"Diary of a Spider"
Student Book pp. 107–129

Be a Reading Detective!

Look back at "Diary of a Spider."

Think about the questions. Look
for clues.

1 **Who** is telling the story?

2 **How** does Spider feel about Fly?

Write your answer.

1 **Who** is telling the story?

_____

_____

_____

_____

_____

Talk about question 2. Tell about the clues you found.

2 **How** does Spider feel about Fly?

noticed

quiet

share

wonderful

The Sandbox

1 I was playing in the park. I **noticed** a new boy.

Have you ever <u>noticed</u> a new student at school? Explain.

_____

_____

_____

2 I did not want to play with him. He was too **quiet**.

Name a place where people need to be <u>quiet</u>.

_____

_____

_____

3 The new boy came over to me. Mom gave me a look. I had to **share** my toys.

What was the last thing that you had to share?

_____

_____

_____

4 The boy's name was Mark. He built a cool castle. We played together. We had a **wonderful** time.

Name something that smells wonderful to you.

_____

_____

_____

The New Playground

by Jason Powe

"I have some **wonderful** news," says Mrs. Ruiz. "You will help plan the new playground!"

"A new playground?" asks Paul.

"That will be fun!" says Rosa.

Stop | **Think** | **Write**

STORY STRUCTURE

What will the children plan?

_____

_____

_____

44

Mrs. Ruiz takes the children to her office. Their teacher, Mr. Jones, is there, too. The room is **quiet**.

"How do we begin?" asks Paul.

Stop **Think** **Write**

The room is not loud. It is

_____.

45

"Think about what you like to do outside," says Mrs. Ruiz. "Then talk about your ideas."

"We all have to agree," says Mr. Jones.

Stop | Think | Write

STORY STRUCTURE

What does Mrs. Ruiz want the children to think about?

_____

_____

_____

_____

46

Each child thinks. Rosa loves to swing. Lucy thinks of shooting hoops. Paul dreams of playing in the sand.

They write down their ideas. Then it is time to **share**.

Stop | Think | Write

VOCABULARY

The children will <u>share</u> their

_____ with each other.

"I **noticed** that we don't have swings," says Rosa. "Let's get some!"

"I want a basketball court," says Lucy.

"A sandbox, too!" says Paul.

Stop **Think** **Write**

Rosa _____ that they don't have swings.

48

Mrs. Ruiz listens. "I like those ideas," she says.

It takes time to build the playground. The children dream about what it will look like.

Stop **Think** **Write**

STORY STRUCTURE

Why does Mrs. Ruiz listen to the children?

_____

_____

_____

49

At last, the playground is ready. It has a sandbox. It has swings. It even has a hoop!

The whole school loves the new playground. The children did a good job.

STORY STRUCTURE

Where are the children at the end of the story?

_____

_____

_____

50

Look Back and Respond

1 What is Mrs. Ruiz's wonderful news?

Hint
For a clue, see page 44.

_____

_____

_____

2 Where do the children meet to plan the playground?

Hint
For a clue, see page 45.

_____

_____

_____

3 Imagine you are planning a playground. What kinds of things would you like?

Hint
Think about what you like to do outside.

_____

_____

_____

Be a Reading Detective!

Return to

Teacher's Pets

Dayle Ann Dodds Illustrated by Marylin Hafner

"Teacher's Pets"
Student Book pp. 147–169

Look back at "Teacher's Pets."

Think about the questions. Look for clues.

1 **Where** does the story take place?

2 **What** animals are in the story?

51A

Write your answer.

1 **Where** does the story take place?

_____

_____

_____

_____

_____

Talk about question 2. Tell about the clues you found.

2 **What** animals are in the story?

Lesson 6

✓ **TARGET VOCABULARY**

branches
deepest
pond
winding

Nature

Check the answer.

1. The river is _____.
It curves left. It curves right.

   ☐ straight ☐ winding ☐ weighed

2. The _____ part of the ocean is almost seven miles below the surface.

   ☐ deepest ☐ busy ☐ winding

3. Frogs and turtles live in water. They could live in a _____.

   ☐ piano ☐ porch ☐ pond

4 What happens to a tree's <u>branches</u> on a windy day?

_____

_____

_____

5 What is the <u>deepest</u> water you have been in?

_____

_____

_____

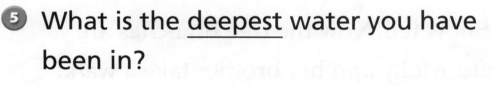

Who Made These?

by John Berry

Snow fell. Now the tree **branches** are white. Molly and her brother take a walk.

"How will we know where to go?" asks Jeff. "Snow has covered the path."

"Don't worry," says Molly. "I can find the way. I know these woods."

Stop · Think · Write

TEXT AND GRAPHIC FEATURES

Who made the tracks in the snow on this page?

_____

_____

_____

They walk across their yard. Jeff stops.
He points to some tracks.

"Who made these?" he asks.

"Here is a hint. It is an animal that
hops," Molly says. "It has a round tail."

Stop **Think** **Write**

TEXT AND GRAPHIC FEATURES

Jeff points to some tracks. The tracks are in the

_____.

"A rabbit?" Jeff asks.

"Right," Molly says. "It was a cottontail rabbit."

They walk into the woods. They go around trees. They go over hills. They go left and right. The path is **winding**.

rabbit

Stop | Think | Write

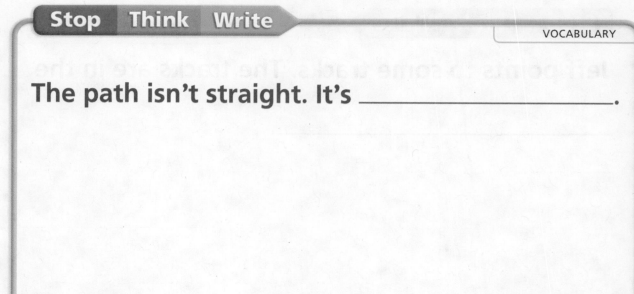

VOCABULARY

The path isn't straight. It's _____.

56

They come to a **pond**. Jeff finds more tracks.

"Who made these?" he asks.

"An animal with a black mask," Molly says. "It has a striped tail."

Stop | Think | Write

TEXT AND GRAPHIC FEATURES

How does the reader know when someone is speaking?

_____

_____

_____

_____

57

"A raccoon?" Jeff asks.

"Right again!" Molly says.

"I saw a raccoon last fall," Jeff says. "It was up in our apple tree. I guess it liked apples."

Molly and Jeff move on.

raccoon

Stop | Think | Write

CAUSE AND EFFECT

Jeff saw a raccoon in a tree. He thought it liked

_____.

They cross a field. Molly points to more tracks.

"These are the **deepest** tracks," Jeff says. "They go far down into the snow. Who made them?"

"A big animal," Molly says. "It has antlers."

Stop Think Write

VOCABULARY

Why do you think these tracks are the deepest?

_____

_____

59

"A deer?" Jeff asks.

"Right again," Molly says. "These are the tracks of a big deer."

"How do you know so much?" Jeff asks.

"I'm older," Molly says. "Soon you'll be a great tracker, too."

deer

Stop | Think | Write

Do you think Molly is a good older sister? Tell why or why not.

_____

_____

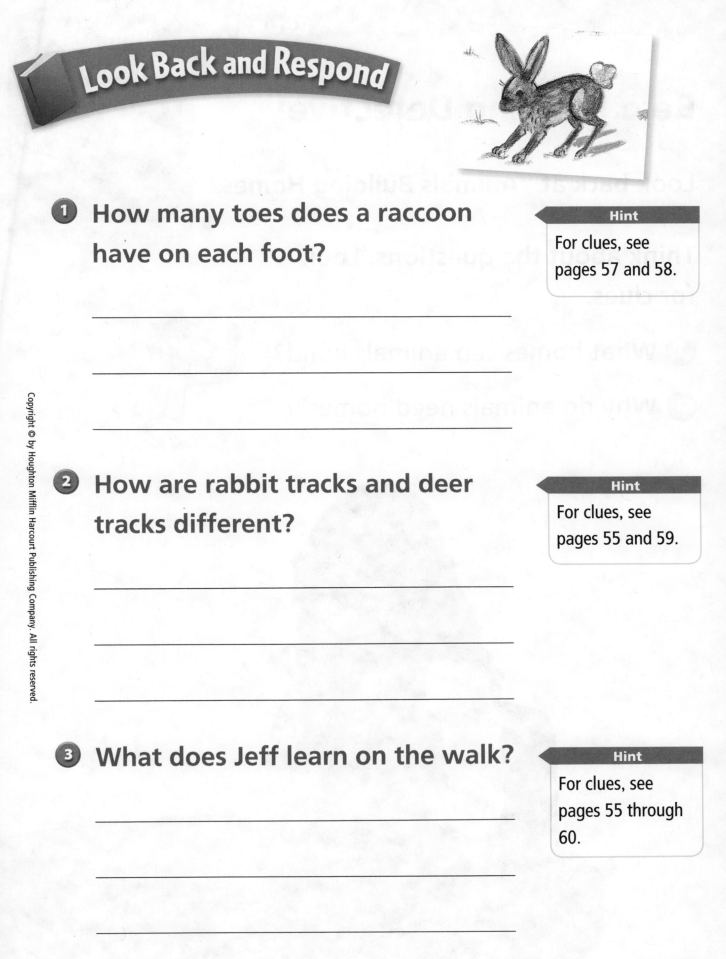

Look Back and Respond

1 How many toes does a raccoon have on each foot?

Hint For clues, see pages 57 and 58.

_____

_____

_____

2 How are rabbit tracks and deer tracks different?

Hint For clues, see pages 55 and 59.

_____

_____

_____

3 What does Jeff learn on the walk?

Hint For clues, see pages 55 through 60.

_____

_____

_____

Return to

Animals Building Homes

"Animals Building Homes"
Student Book pp. 191–205

Be a Reading Detective!

Look back at "Animals Building Homes."

Think about the questions. Look
for clues.

1 **What** homes can animals build?

2 **Why** do animals need homes?

Write your answer.

1 **What** homes can animals build?

_____

_____

_____

_____

Talk about question 2. Tell about the clues you found.

2 **Why** do animals need homes?

61B

blooming

plain

scent

shovels

In the Garden

1 Roses are **blooming** in the garden. New flowers grow each year.

What season is it when flowers and trees are <u>blooming</u>?

_____

_____

_____

2 The roses have a sweet **scent**. Many people like to smell them.

Name something outside that has a sweet <u>scent</u>.

_____

_____

_____

3 The apple tree looks **plain** in winter. It does not have leaves or flowers. The tree blooms in spring. Then it looks dressed up!

Name two things that can look plain.

_____

_____

_____

4 In the garden, people use **shovels**. They are good for breaking up the dirt.

What are some jobs that <u>shovels</u> could help you do?

_____

_____

_____

Rosa's Garden

by Carol Alexander

I am Sofia. This is Miss Rosa.

She has a garden. It is big!

Miss Rosa grows flowers.

She grows carrots and peas.

I don't eat peas. Not one pea.

No way!

Stop Think Write

CONCLUSIONS

Who do you think planted the garden? Why?

_____

_____

_____

This summer, Miss Rosa fell. She hurt her knee. Now she can't walk. She just sits in a chair. She watches the birds.

Two **shovels** lie in the grass. Miss Rosa looks sad. What would help her feel better?

Stop **Think** **Write**

INFER AND PREDICT

What could help Miss Rosa feel better?

_____

_____

_____

I go home to think. "Mom, I need paper. I want to draw a picture."

Mom smiles. "Here is some **plain** white paper." She gives me a few pieces. "I can't wait to see what you draw."

Stop | Think | Write

VOCABULARY

Sofia's paper has no lines. It is

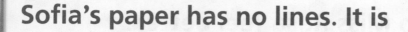

I find my crayons. What will I draw?
I close my eyes. The **scent** of flowers
blows in through the window. Now I
know just what to draw.

Stop Think Write

What do you think Sofia will draw?

_____

_____

_____

I draw and draw. Here are the sweet peas. They are **blooming** in May. There are the tomatoes. They are red and round.

I keep drawing. Mom says, "Your hand will fall off, Sofia!"

VOCABULARY

The flowers are _____ in Sofia's picture.

At last, I am done. I find Miss Rosa.
I hand her my picture.

"This is for you," I say.

She looks at it. She smiles and
hugs me.

"Do you really like it?" I ask.

Stop **Think** **Write**

CONCLUSIONS

Does Miss Rosa like the drawing? Explain.

_____

_____

_____

"Oh, yes!" Miss Rosa says. "This is the best garden. It makes me happy. Thank you, Sofia."

"Spring will come again. We can work in the garden together," I say. "We will plant lots of peas!"

Stop **Think** **Write**

The picture makes Miss Rosa feel

_____ .

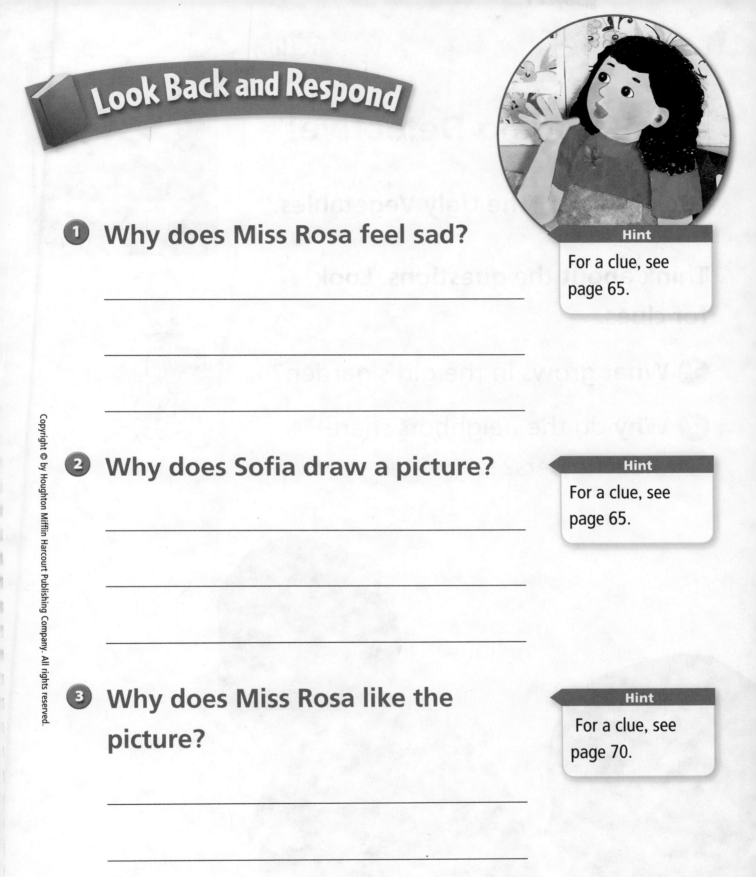

Look Back and Respond

1 Why does Miss Rosa feel sad?

_____

_____

_____

Hint

For a clue, see page 65.

2 Why does Sofia draw a picture?

_____

_____

_____

Hint

For a clue, see page 65.

3 Why does Miss Rosa like the picture?

_____

_____

_____

Hint

For a clue, see page 70.

Return to

Be a Reading Detective!

Look back at "The Ugly Vegetables."

"The Ugly Vegetables"
Student Book pp. 227–249

Think about the questions. Look for clues.

1 **What** grows in the girl's garden?

2 **Why** do the neighbors share their flowers?

Write your answer.

1 **What** grows in the girl's garden?

_____

_____

_____

_____

_____

Talk about question 2. Tell about the clues you found.

2 **Why** do the neighbors share their flowers?

Lesson

8

✓ **TARGET VOCABULARY**

beware

damage

pounding

prevent

When a Storm Comes

1. Storms can come fast. _____ of strong winds! Watch out for dark clouds. They bring rain.

2. Storms can _____ buildings. Windows can break. A roof can blow off!

3 _____ rain hits the ground hard. Flowers are knocked over. Tree branches break.

4 We can take steps to _____ a storm from hurting us. We can stay inside. We can stay away from windows and doors.

Write the vocabulary word that best completes the synonym web.

5

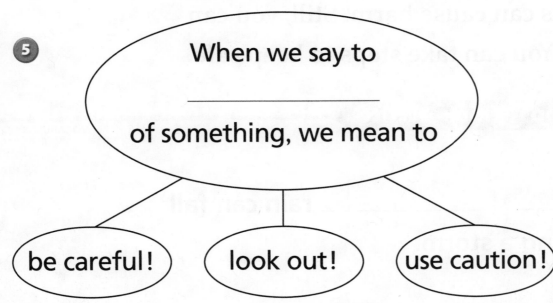

When we say to

_____

of something, we mean to

be careful!   look out!   use caution!

Keeping Safe in a Storm

by Carol Alexander

Big storms can be scary. Strong winds are loud. They shake things. **Pounding** rain falls.

Storms can cause harm. Still, you can prepare. You can take steps to keep safe.

Stop | Think | Write

VOCABULARY

A _____ rain can fall during a storm.

74

Planning

You should plan ahead. Find safe places at home. They should be away from windows and doors.

You may need supplies. You can put water in bottles. You can freeze food. Make sure you have candles, too.

| Stop | Think | Write |

MAIN IDEAS AND DETAILS

Storing _____ in bottles can be part of a plan for staying safe.

Before a Storm

You can learn about a storm that is coming. Just listen to the TV or radio. Experts watch the path of storms. News reporters warn people about bad storms.

Some storms are very strong. It may not be safe to stay at home. You may have to go to a safer place.

Stop Think Write

If a storm is very _____,
you may not be able to stay at home.

You can **prevent** problems at home. Bring toys and pets inside. Put garbage cans where wind can't tip them over.

Wind can **damage** windows. Some people tape windows. Tape makes them stronger.

Stop Think Write

Storms can _____ windows.
Taping windows helps to protect them.

During a Storm

The storm hits! You should not go outside. Find a safe place inside.

You can play games. Don't play games that use electricity. Things that use electricity can be dangerous in storms. **Beware** of computers. Do not talk on the phone.

Stop   Think   Write

MAIN IDEAS AND DETAILS

Games that don't use _____ are safe to play during a storm.

After a Storm

Listen to the news. Reporters will tell you when it is safe to go outside.

You must still be careful. Stay away from damaged trees. Ask a grownup where you can play.

Isn't it good to be outside again?

Stop **Think** **Write**

MAIN IDEAS AND DETAILS

Listen to the _____ to find out when it is safe to go outside after a storm.

Kinds of Storms

A **blizzard** is a bad winter storm. It has big winds. It has lots of snow.

A **tornado** is a tube of wind. It can pick up a house!

A **hurricane** is a storm from the sea. It has big winds and waves. It can cause bad floods.

Stop | Think | Write

COMPARE AND CONTRAST

Write one way all these storms are alike.

_____

_____

_____

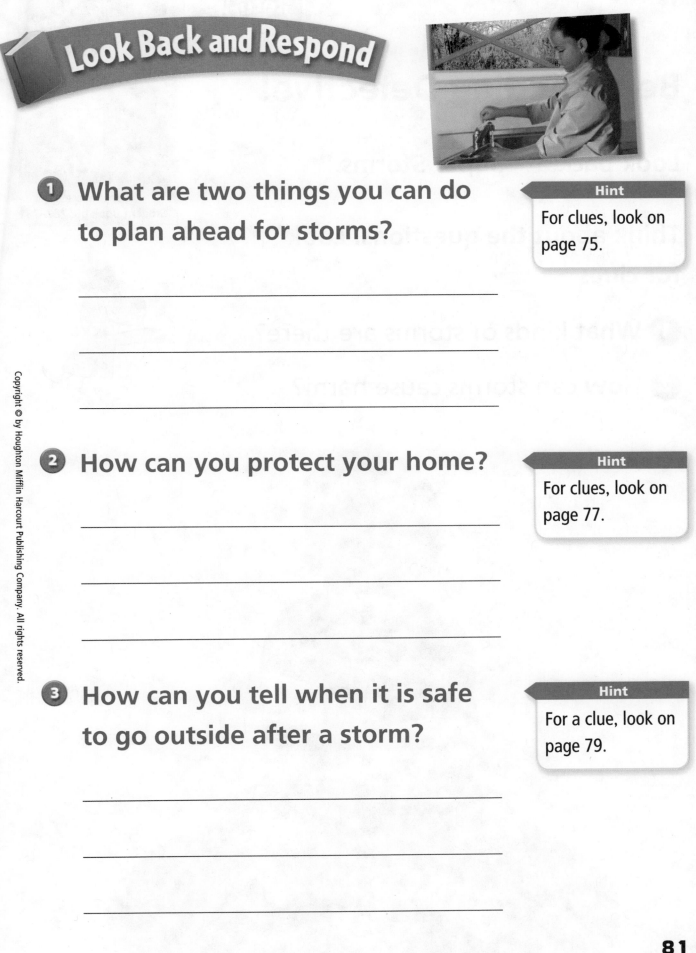

Look Back and Respond

1 What are two things you can do to plan ahead for storms?

Hint
For clues, look on page 75.

_____

_____

_____

2 How can you protect your home?

Hint
For clues, look on page 77.

_____

_____

_____

3 How can you tell when it is safe to go outside after a storm?

Hint
For a clue, look on page 79.

_____

_____

_____

Be a Reading Detective!

Return to

SUPER STORMS

"Super Storms"
Student Book pp. 267–281

Look back at "Super Storms."

Think about the questions. Look
for clues.

1 **What** kinds of storms are there?

2 **How** can storms cause harm?

81A

Write your answer.

1 **What** kinds of storms are there?

_____

_____

_____

_____

_____

Talk about question 2. Tell about the clues you found.

2 **How** can storms cause harm?

curled

direction

height

toward

A Forest

1 A forest is full of trees. The **height** of each tree is different. Some trees are taller than others.

Name something with a height that's greater than your school's.

_____

_____

_____

2 There are other plants in a forest. Vines are **curled** around the trees.

Name an animal that you've seen curled up.

_____

_____

3 There are animals in the forest. It is hard to see them. People scare them. Then the animals run in a different **direction**.

Name two things that would make you run in a different <u>direction</u>.

_____

_____

_____

4 You may see an animal in the forest. Be quiet. Be still. Don't move **toward** it.

Why isn't it a good idea to move <u>toward</u> a wild animal?

_____

_____

_____

Tortoise Gets a Home

by Jake Harris

Forest loved the animals. She gave each one a home.

Lizard got a rock home. Crab got a hole in the sand. Forest forgot all about Tortoise.

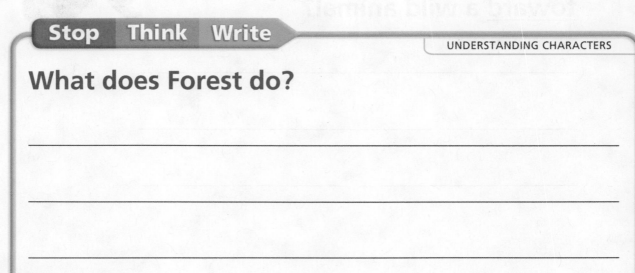

Stop **Think** **Write**

UNDERSTANDING CHARACTERS

What does Forest do?

84

Snake **curled** up under leaves. Owl sat in a hole in a tree.

The animals thanked Forest. They were all happy. All but Tortoise! Tortoise was sad.

Stop | **Think** | **Write**

Snake likes to be _____ up in his home.

One night, a storm came. Tortoise had no home. He needed to find one. He needed to stay warm and dry.

Tortoise saw a hole in some rocks. Lizard looked out. "Sorry, my house is too small for you," she said.

CAUSE AND EFFECT

Why can't Lizard share her house with Tortoise?

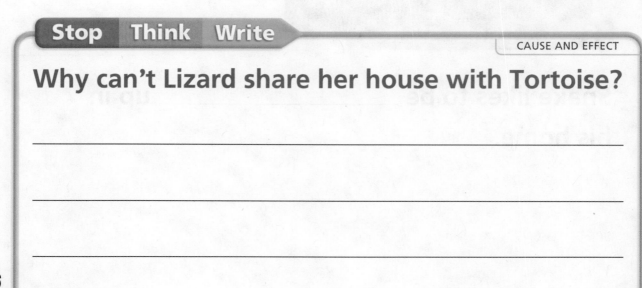

Tortoise walked **toward** a hole in the sand. Crab popped his head out.

Tortoise tried to crawl under some leaves. "I'm under here!" said Snake.

Stop | **Think** | **Write**

VOCABULARY

Tortoise walks _____

Crab's home.

Tortoise went in the **direction** of a tall tree. Owl hooted at him to go away. The tree was the right **height** for Owl. It was too tall for Tortoise.

Tortoise did not want to be in the rain. Then he found a broken coconut shell.

Stop   Think   Write

UNDERSTANDING CHARACTERS

Tortoise does not want _____.

Tortoise crawled under the shell. He pulled in his legs. He pulled in his neck. It was just big enough to cover him. Tortoise was warm and dry.

In the morning, the rain had gone. Tortoise came out from his shell. Forest saw him.

Stop | **Think** | **Write**

STORY STRUCTURE

What does Tortoise do during the storm?

_____

_____

_____

"Tortoise!" said Forest. "I am sorry. I forgot to give you a home. I see you found one. This shell will stay on your back. Your home will always be with you."

Today, all tortoises have shells.

Forest is _____ she forgot about Tortoise.

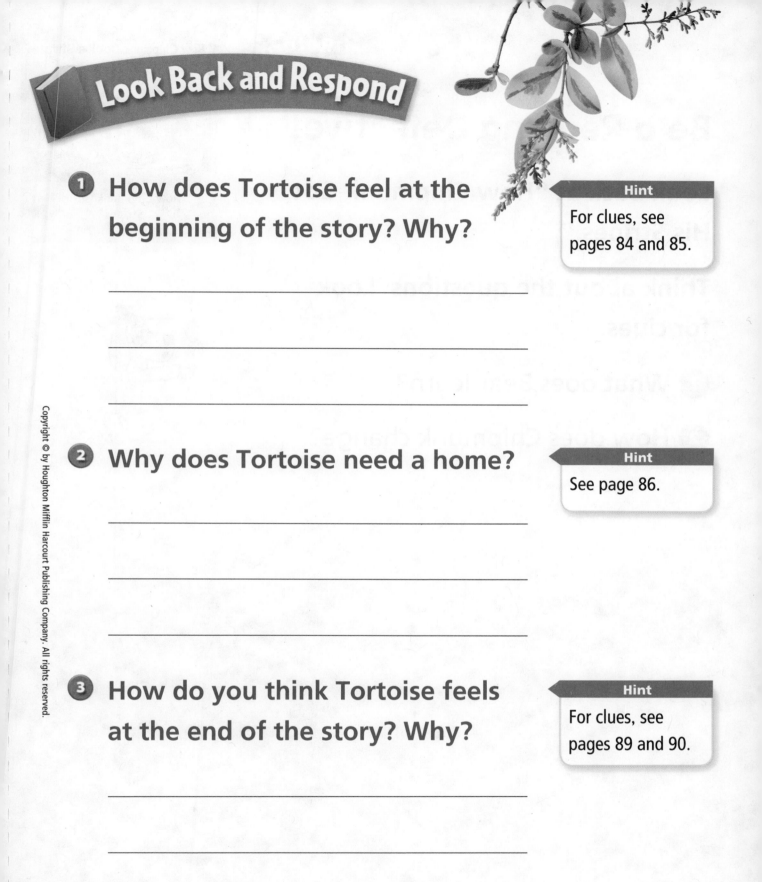

Look Back and Respond

1 How does Tortoise feel at the beginning of the story? Why?

Hint

For clues, see pages 84 and 85.

_____

_____

_____

2 Why does Tortoise need a home?

Hint

See page 86.

_____

_____

_____

3 How do you think Tortoise feels at the end of the story? Why?

Hint

For clues, see pages 89 and 90.

_____

_____

_____

Return to

"How Chipmunk Got His Stripes"
Student Book pp. 299–319

Be a Reading Detective!

Look back at "How Chipmunk Got His Stripes."

Think about the questions. Look for clues.

1 **What** does Bear learn?

2 **How** does Chipmunk change?

Write your answer.

1 **What** does Bear learn?

_____

_____

_____

_____

Talk about question 2. Tell about the clues you found.

2 **How** does Chipmunk change?

✓ **TARGET VOCABULARY**

choices

disgusting

millions

weaker

Trash in Our Oceans

Check the answer.

1 _____ of plastic bags go into the ocean. They hurt animals that live there.

☐ **Muscles**

☐ **Weaker**

☐ **Millions**

2 Trash in the ocean is _____. It traps fish. It makes them sick.

☐ **screaming**

☐ **disgusting**

☐ **weaker**

3 A fish can get stuck in a bag. The fish can get hurt. It cannot find food. The fish gets _____.

☐ **millions** ☐ **direction** ☐ **weaker**

4 What are some <u>choices</u> that you have today?

_____

_____

_____

5 Name something that you can count in the <u>millions</u>.

_____

At the Beach

by John Berry

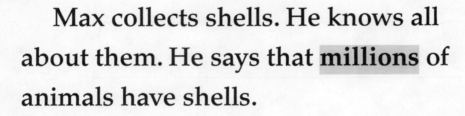

Max collects shells. He knows all about them. He says that **millions** of animals have shells.

He takes me to the beach. Max is excited. He wants to find a conch shell.

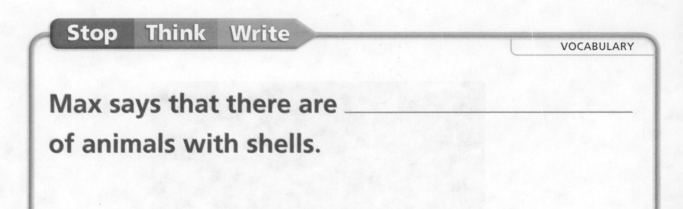

Stop | **Think** | **Write**

VOCABULARY

Max says that there are _____

of animals with shells.

94

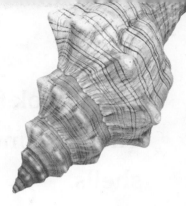

We get to the beach. Max gets upset.
He finds trash in the sand.

"This is **disgusting**!" he says. "People
should not litter."

I agree.

Stop Think Write

VOCABULARY

Trash on a beach isn't nice. Max thinks it is

_____.

We look for shells. First we find rocks. Then we find sticks. At last we find shells.

"Look at this one," I say.

"I have one like that," Max says. "See?"

MAIN IDEAS AND DETAILS

The boys find _____ at the beach.

He pulls a shell from his bag. It is the same. I toss my shell into the sea.

"Hey! A crab!" I say.

"It has two claws," Max says. "The big one is strong. The small one is **weaker**."

Stop **Think** **Write**

FACT AND OPINION

One fact about the crab is that it has

_____.

"There's another crab," I say. "It looks funny."

"That's a hermit crab," says Max. "They find shells to live in. This crab doesn't have a shell."

"You can give him a shell," I say.

FACT AND OPINION

The boy says that the crab looks funny. Is that a fact or an opinion?

_____

_____

98

"Hermit crabs live in snail shells," says Max. "I have only one snail shell."

"Well, you have two **choices**," I say. "You can give the crab a home or keep the shell."

Stop **Think** **Write**

FACT AND OPINION

Max says that hermit crabs live in snail shells. Is that a fact or an opinion?

_____

_____

I walk away. I look back. Max puts the shell on the sand. The crab goes in. Max looks happy.

I'm happy, too.

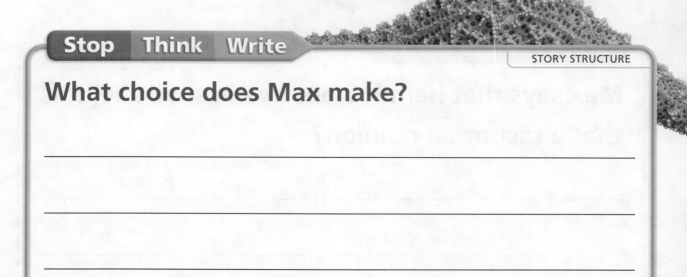

Stop | **Think** | **Write**

What choice does Max make?

_____

_____

_____

Look Back and Respond

1 Look at page 95. Write one sentence that is an opinion.

Hint

Remember that an opinion shows what someone thinks or feels.

_____

_____

_____

2 Write one fact that Max tells about shells.

Hint

For clues, see pages 94, 98, and 99.

_____

_____

_____

3 If you were Max, which choice would you have made?

Hint

Think about Max's choices. Think about what Max wants.

_____

_____

_____

Be a Reading Detective!

Return to

THE LIFE OF JELLYFISH
Twig C. George

"Jellies"
Student Book pp. 337–353

Look back at "Jellies."

Think about the questions. Look
for clues.

1 **What** would life be like as a jellyfish?

2 **How** does the author feel about
jellyfish?

Write your answer.

1 **What** would life be like as a jellyfish?

_____

_____

_____

_____

_____

Talk about question 2. Tell about the clues you found.

2 **How** does the author feel about jellyfish?

believe

furious

impossible

problem

Getting Along

1 Mia wants to draw a cat. Leo shows her how. He breaks her chalk. Now Mia is very mad.

She is _____

with Leo.

2 Leo says, "I'm very sorry. I can't fix your chalk. That's

_____."

Mia feels better. "I

_____ you," she

says. "I know you are sorry."

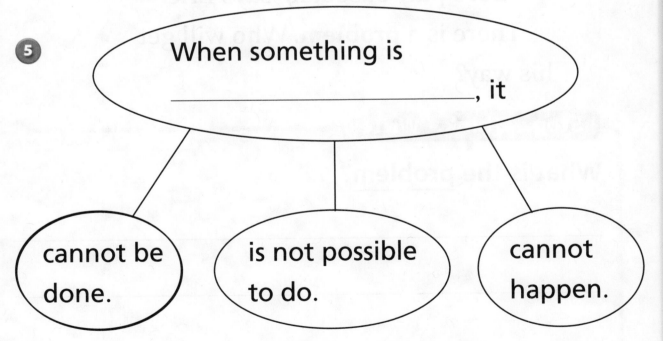

4 "I can fix the

_____," Leo tells

Mia. He gives her his chalk.

Write the vocabulary word that best completes the synonym web.

5

When something is

_____, it

cannot be done.

is not possible to do.

cannot happen.

The Play Date

by Margaret Maugenest

Eric and Dylan are brothers. Raul comes to play with them.

"Let's make a spaceship," says Dylan.

"Let's play baseball," says Eric.

There is a **problem**. Who will get his way?

Stop | **Think** | **Write**

VOCABULARY

What is the problem?

_____

_____

_____

"I have an idea," says Raul. "Let's build a spaceship first. Then we can play ball."

Eric gets **furious**. "No," he says. "Making a spaceship is a baby game."

Eric goes to his room. He slams the door.

Stop **Think** **Write**

CONCLUSIONS

How can you tell that Eric is mad?

_____

_____

_____

105

Raul frowns. "Let's make the spaceship. Eric will calm down. He can come later," Raul says.

Dylan and Raul go to Dylan's room. Eric hears them laugh. He puts his ear to the wall.

Stop **Think** **Write**

CONCLUSIONS

Two friends, _____ and

_____ , are having a good

time.

Eric hears talking.

"This is fun," says Raul.

"I wish Eric were here," says Dylan.

Eric wants to play. It is **impossible** for him to stay mad. He goes to Dylan's room. He peeks inside.

Stop **Think** **Write**

VOCABULARY

It is _____ for Eric to stay angry.

Eric sees the spaceship. Dylan and Raul are in it.

"Blast off!" says Dylan.

"Is there room for me?" says Eric.

Stop **Think** **Write**

CONCLUSIONS

What does Eric want to do?

_____

_____

_____

Dylan and Raul smile.

"Yes! Get in," says Raul. "We're off to the moon."

Eric sits in the tent. "I'm sorry I got mad," he says.

Stop	Think	Write

CONCLUSIONS

Dylan and Raul feel _____ when Eric comes.

"We didn't **believe** you would stay mad," says Raul.

"We'll play ball soon. We just have to get back from the moon!" says Dylan.

Stop | Think | Write

STORY STRUCTURE

They will all play _____ later.

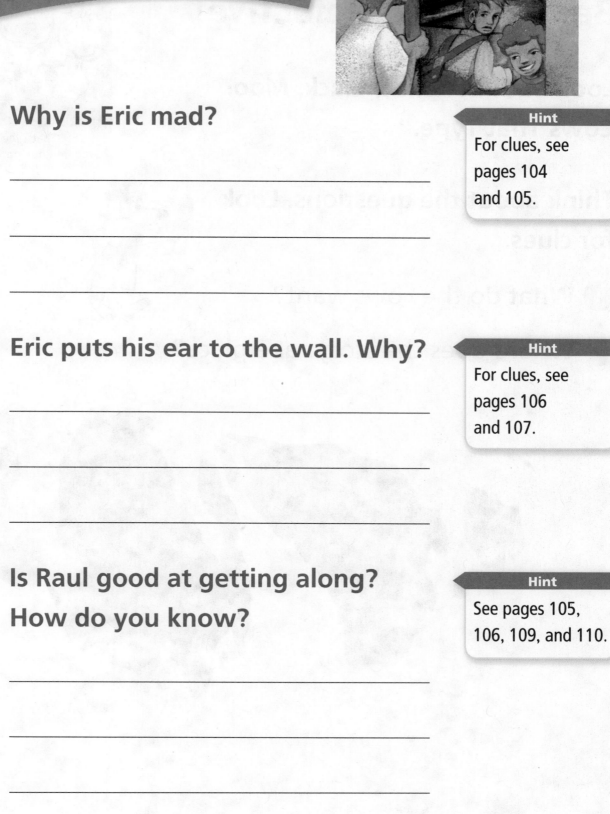

Look Back and Respond

1 **Why is Eric mad?**

Hint

For clues, see pages 104 and 105.

_____

_____

_____

2 **Eric puts his ear to the wall. Why?**

Hint

For clues, see pages 106 and 107.

_____

_____

_____

3 **Is Raul good at getting along? How do you know?**

Hint

See pages 105, 106, 109, and 110.

_____

_____

_____

Return to

CLICK, CLACK, MOO
Cows That Type
Doreen Cronin pictures by Betsy Lewin

"Click, Clack, Moo: Cows
That Type"
Student Book pp. 375–393

Be a Reading Detective!

Look back at "Click, Clack, Moo:
Cows That Type."

Think about the questions. Look
for clues.

1. **What** do the cows want?

2. **Where** does the story take place?

Write your answer.

1 **What** do the cows want?

_____

_____

_____

_____

_____

Talk about question 2. Tell about the clues you found.

2 **Where** does the story take place?

✓ **TARGET VOCABULARY**

concentrate

performance

tune

volume

Music at School

Our music teacher is Mr. Valentine. We listen carefully when he plays a new **tune** on the piano.

Mr. Valentine reminds us about **volume**. He tells us when to sing quietly and when to sing full out!

We **concentrate** as we learn a new rhythm on the drums. Ba ba boom, ba ba boom, ba ba boom boom BOOM!

We are getting ready for a **performance**. Our parents will come to hear us sing and play. I can't wait!

 If the _____ on the radio is too loud, you can turn it down.

 We bought tickets to see the _____.

 Sometimes I get a _____ stuck in my head. It goes around and around all day.

 When is it important for you to <u>concentrate</u>? Give an example and explain why.

_____

_____

_____

Musical Instruments

by Mia Lewis

Music is fun to hear, and even more fun to play! One day you may get to pick an instrument to learn. Read about the different kinds so you can make a good choice.

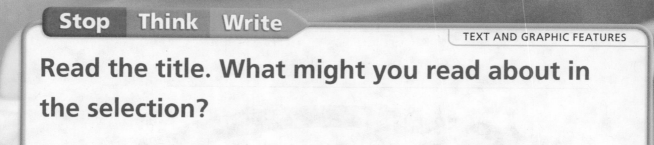

Stop | Think | Write

TEXT AND GRAPHIC FEATURES

Read the title. What might you read about in the selection?

_____

_____

claves

Percussion Instruments

Do you like to bang and crash? Do you like to rattle and shake? Do you like to bash and boom? If you do, a percussion instrument might be just right for you.

maracas

Stop Think Write

TEXT AND GRAPHIC FEATURES

Look at the illustrations on the page. Name two percussion instruments.

_____

_____

WIND INSTRUMENTS

If you blow into it and it makes a noise, it's a wind instrument. A whistle and a kazoo are wind instruments. So are flutes and recorders.

Stop | **Think** | **Write**

CAUSE AND EFFECT

What creates the sound in a wind instrument?

_____

_____

_____

Brass Instruments

Trumpets, tubas, and trombones are brass instruments—one family of wind instruments. They are good for playing at a high **volume**. Hear them in a marching band!

tuba

Stop	Think	Write

TEXT AND GRAPHIC FEATURES

How does the heading on this page help you to understand what you are reading?

_____

_____

String Instruments

A violin is a string instrument. So is a guitar. A cello is, too. You use a bow or pluck with your fingers to play a **tune**.

violin

Stop   Think   Write

COMPARE AND CONTRAST

How are string instruments different from wind instruments?

_____

_____

_____

No Instrument?

Don't like any of these? That's OK. Sing, clap, stamp, or snap. You can be your own instrument. Or grab a pot and a spoon. Get creative. Make your own!

Stop | Think | Write

INFER/PREDICT

What "instrument" does the author think you will make with a pot and a spoon?

_____

_____

On Stage

It is fun to see a musical **performance**. It is even more fun to play in one! Practice hard. **Concentrate** in music class. You will soon be on stage!

INFER/PREDICT

Is learning an instrument well enough to perform on stage easy or difficult?

_____

_____

120

Look Back and Respond

1 **Name two wind instruments.**

Hint

See pages 116 and 117 for clues.

_____

_____

_____

2 **What are two ways string instruments are played?**

Hint

See page 118 for clues.

_____

_____

_____

3 **How can a person be a musical instrument?**

Hint

See page 119 for a clue.

_____

_____

_____

Return to

"Ah, Music!"
Student Book pp. 411–421

Be a Reading Detective!

Look back at "Ah, Music!"

Think about the questions. Look for clues.

1 **What** is music?

2 **How** do people make music?

Write your answer.

1 **What** is music?

_____

_____

_____

_____

Talk about question 2. Tell about the clues you found.

2 **How** do people make music?

✓ **TARGET VOCABULARY**

community

culture

special

wear

Ball Games

1 Kids like to play with balls. You can bounce a ball. You can throw a ball. All the kids in a **community** can play.

What kinds of ball games do kids in your community play?

_____

_____

_____

2 Ball games are part of a culture. Music and food are part of a **culture**, too.

Name a food that is part of your culture.

_____

3 Players **wear** uniforms in many ball games.

What is your favorite thing to <u>wear</u>?

_____

_____

_____

4 Dodge ball is a game. It has **special** rules. You can hit someone with the ball. Then the person is out.

What are the <u>special</u> rules of your favorite game?

_____

_____

_____

Game Time!

by John Berry

What games do you play? Do you play with a ball? Do you play board games?

Kids play all over the world. Every **culture** has its own games. There are many ways to have fun!

Stop | Think | Write

VOCABULARY

Games are part of a country's

_____.

Mancala

Mancala is a counting game. It was first played in Africa. You can play with seeds. You can play with stones.

Players pick up the stones. They drop them into the bins. It seems easy, but it is hard to play well!

Stop | **Think** | **Write**

MAIN IDEA AND DETAILS

You can play mancala with

_____.

Pachisi

Pachisi comes from India. Players move pieces on a board. Each player wants to get to the middle first.

Long ago, rulers in India played pachisi. Today, people play in other countries, too.

Stop **Think** **Write**

Pachisi is played with pieces on a

_____.

Games with String

The Inuit are native people. They are from North America. People in the Inuit **community** learn to make string shapes. It is their tradition.

Children all over play games with string. Cat's cradle is one string game.

Stop **Think** **Write**

MAIN IDEA AND DETAILS

The Inuit people learn to make shapes with

_____.

Soccer

People all over the world play soccer. More people play soccer than any other game!

Players run. They kick the ball. They cannot touch it with their hands. Players often **wear** uniforms.

Stop | Think | Write

VOCABULARY

Soccer players can _____ uniforms.

128

A Battle Game

A game was invented in China. It is hundreds of years old. It is played with stones on a board. The game is called Go.

The game is a battle. Players trap each other's stones. They must plan well. It takes skill to win!

Stop **Think** **Write**

CONCLUSIONS

In the game Go, players trap each other's stones. It is like a _____.

129

Marbles

Long ago, children in Egypt played a game with marbles. Kids still play marbles today. Kids collect marbles, too.

Marbles come in many colors. Some **special** marbles are called cat's eyes. They sparkle like the eyes of a cat.

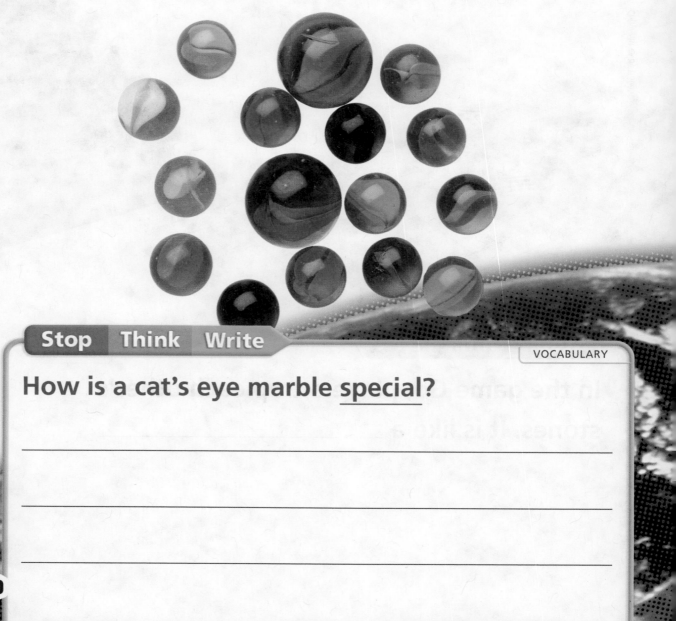

Stop **Think** **Write**

VOCABULARY

How is a cat's eye marble special?

_____

_____

_____

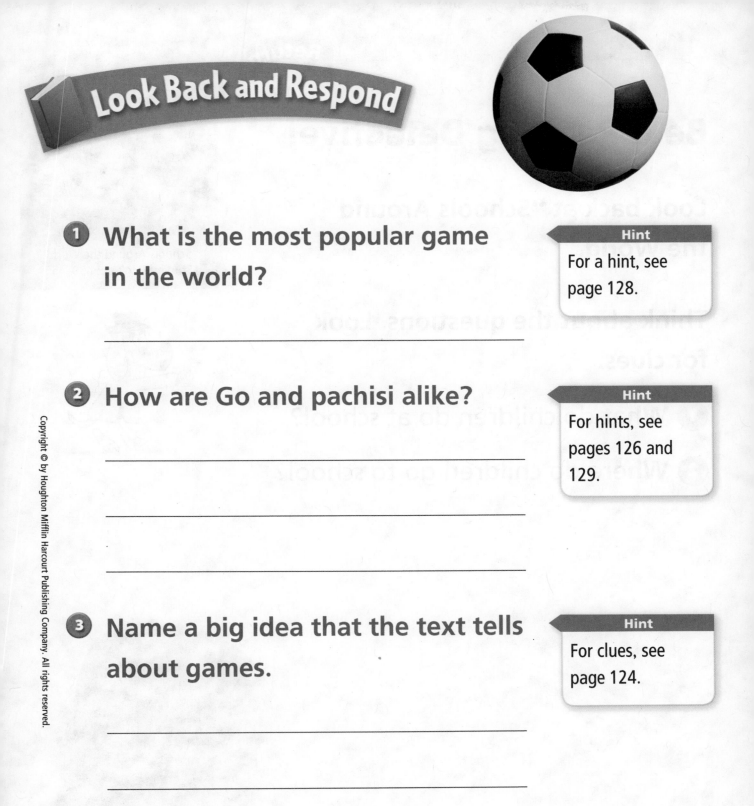

Look Back and Respond

1 What is the most popular game in the world?

Hint

For a hint, see page 128.

_____

2 How are Go and pachisi alike?

Hint

For hints, see pages 126 and 129.

_____

_____

_____

3 Name a big idea that the text tells about games.

Hint

For clues, see page 124.

_____

_____

_____

Be a Reading Detective!

Around the World

Schools

"Schools Around the World"
Student Book pp. 439–455

Look back at "Schools Around
the World."

Think about the questions. Look
for clues.

1 **What** do children do at school?

2 **Where** do children go to school?

Write your answer.

1 **What** do children do at school?

_____

_____

_____

_____

_____

_____

Talk about question 2. Tell about the clues you found.

2 **Where** do children go to school?

The Senses

curious

darkness

knowledge

motion

1 The five senses are sight, hearing, smell, taste, and touch. They give us **knowledge** of the world.

What <u>knowledge</u> can you get from hearing something?

_____

_____

_____

2 When we are **curious** about something, we use our senses. We look, listen, feel, or smell to learn more.

What are you <u>curious</u> about?

_____

_____

_____

3 You are swimming at the beach. You see the water. You taste the salt. You hear the ocean. You feel the **motion** of the waves.

What other motion might you see at the beach?

_____

_____

_____

4 You can hear things at night. You can feel and smell at night. You might not see well in the **darkness**.

Write a word that means the opposite of darkness.

_____

Louis Braille

by Karen Bischoff

Louis Braille was born about two hundred years ago. He became blind at the age of three. He lived in a world of **darkness** from then on.

Louis was smart. He tried to do well at school. However, he could not read. He could not write. Louis had to leave school. Still, he wanted to learn.

Stop · Think · Write

CAUSE AND EFFECT

The author tells you that school was hard for Louis. That is because Louis was

_____.

A Special School

Louis got a lucky break. He joined a special school. It was for children who could not see. He learned a lot there.

Louis was **curious**. He wanted to learn more. He wanted the **knowledge** he could get from books.

Stop **Think** **Write**

VOCABULARY

Louis wanted to read books. This shows that he

was _____.

Louis Gets an Idea

Louis was blind, but he could feel with his fingers. He had an idea to make writing that people could feel. He thought of letters made of dots. They would be little bumps on the paper.

Stop **Think** **Write**

Tell why Louis wanted to write letters made of dots.

_____

_____

_____

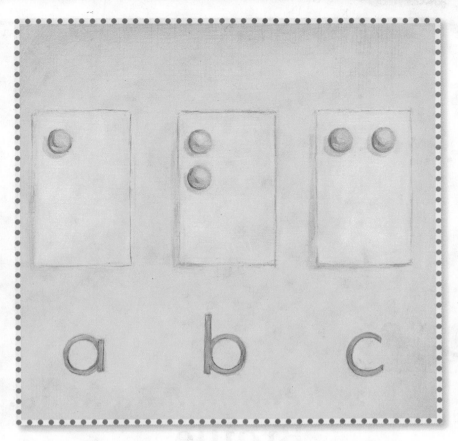

Louis took paper. He made little bumps on it. Each set of bumps was a letter. When he joined the letters, he made words. Louis was writing!

Louis made a **motion** over the bumps with his fingers. He could feel the bumps. He was reading with his hands!

Stop　Think　Write

VOCABULARY

Tell about the hand motion Louis made.

_____

_____

_____

137

Braille

Louis was only 15 years old. He made an alphabet for blind people. That alphabet is now called braille.

His idea let him write. It let other blind people read what he wrote. He started to make books written in braille.

Stop **Think** **Write**

MAIN IDEA AND DETAILS

Who needed Louis's alphabet?

_____

_____

_____

Helping Others

Louis stayed at the school. He became a teacher. He showed children how to read in braille. He showed them how to write in braille.

The children loved Louis. He opened the door to a new world for them.

Stop **Think** **Write**

INFER/PREDICT

What is the new world that Louis gave to the children?

_____

_____

_____

139

Braille Today

Today, you can find braille books in stores and in libraries. People all over the world read braille.

Many people cannot see. Thanks to Louis Braille, they can read and write.

Stop | Think | Write

Why do people today remember Louis Braille?

_____

_____

_____

140

1 **Why do you think the author told you that Louis Braille was blind?**

Hint

You must read every page to answer this.

_____

_____

2 **What is braille?**

Hint

For clues, see pages 138 and 139.

_____

_____

3 **Did the author write "Louis Braille" to entertain you or to give you information?**

Hint

Did you learn something new?

_____

_____

_____

Be a Reading Detective!

"Helen Keller"
Student Book pp. 473–489

Look back at "Helen Keller."

Think about the questions. Look for clues.

1 **Who** was Helen Keller?

2 **What** did Annie teach Helen?

Write your answer.

1 **Who** was Helen Keller?

_____

_____

_____

_____

_____

Talk about question 2. Tell about the clues you found.

2 **What** did Annie teach Helen?

buddy

safety

speech

station

Safety at the Beach

1. Lifeguards work at the beach. They watch the swimmers from a **station**.

   Name another kind of station.

   _____

2. A lifeguard gave a **speech**. She told us how to be safe in the ocean.

   Think about a speech you would like to give. What would you talk about?

   _____

   _____

   _____

3 Don't take chances at the beach. Stay out of danger. Follow the **safety** rules.

Name a good _safety_ rule for the beach.

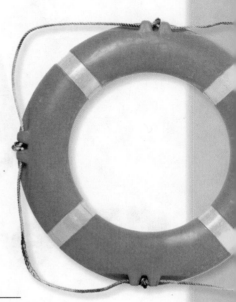

_____

_____

4 You should never swim alone. Always swim with a **buddy**.

What is something you like to do with a _buddy_?

_____

_____

_____

Fire Safety Day

by John Berry

Randy walked to school. He was glad.
His class had gym today. He loved gym.
They would play games. They would
kick balls. Best of all, they would tumble.
Randy was ready to practice somersaults
and cartwheels.

Stop Think Write

UNDERSTANDING CHARACTERS

Randy is excited to go to school because he

wants to _____.

When he got to the gym, the gray mats were not out. They were stacked against the wall.

Mrs. Nelson was standing with two people from the fire **station**.

"Good morning," she said. "Today we have a special treat."

Stop Think Write

CONCLUSIONS

Who is standing with Mrs. Nelson?

_____

_____

_____

145

"These firefighters will talk to us about fire **safety**," said Mrs. Nelson. "They will teach us some rules. We will learn how to avoid fires. We will also learn what to do if there is a fire."

Randy was sad. He liked gym a lot. Now he would have to wait until next week.

Stop **Think** **Write**

Randy's class is going to learn about fire

_____.

Ingrid came over. She was Randy's **buddy.** "What's wrong?" Ingrid said.

"Why do we have to learn about fire safety?" Randy said. "That's no fun."

"It may not be fun," she said. "Still, it's good to know."

"Maybe," he said. "I wanted to do tumbling today."

Stop	Think	Write

CAUSE AND EFFECT

Why is Randy sad?

_____

_____

_____

147

"Good morning," Chief Sims said. "We want you to be safe. The best rule is to avoid fires. Don't play with matches. They start fires."

Officer Jones gave a **speech** about smoke alarms. "Every house needs a smoke alarm," she said. "They save lives."

Stop | Think | Write

VOCABULARY

Officer Jones talks to the class.
Her _____ is about smoke alarms.

"Now let's learn what to do if your clothes catch on fire," said Officer Jones. She pulled out the gray mats. "First, stop moving. Then drop to the floor. Then roll back and forth. Who wants to try?"

Randy tried "stop, drop, and roll." It was just like tumbling!

Stop | **Think** | **Write**

STORY STRUCTURE

Randy gets to roll on the

_____.

149

At recess, Ingrid played with Randy. "We learned a lot about fire safety today," she said.

"I learned something else," said Randy.

"What's that?" Ingrid asked.

"It was more fun than I thought!" he said.

Stop | Think | Write

UNDERSTANDING CHARACTERS

Randy has _____ learning about fire safety.

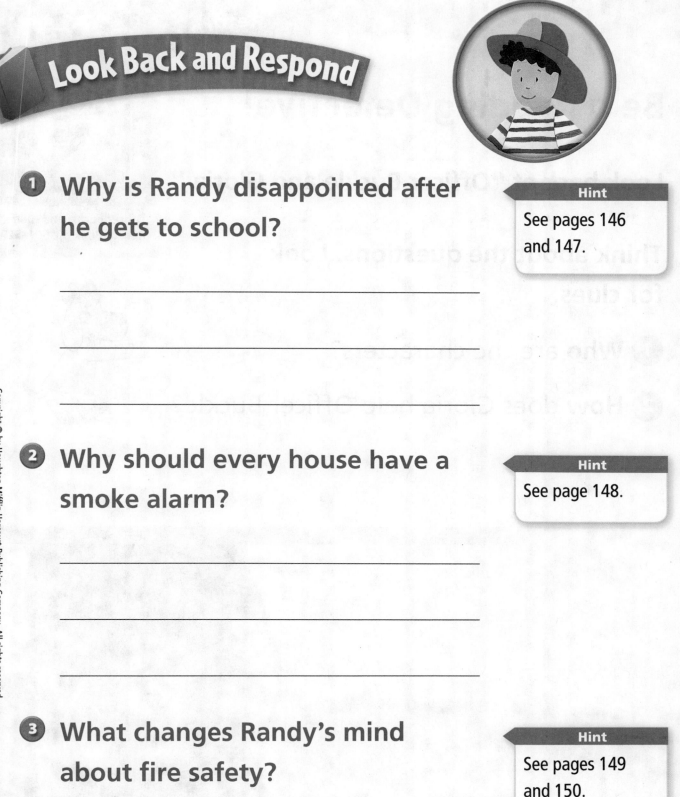

Look Back and Respond

1 Why is Randy disappointed after he gets to school?

Hint
See pages 146 and 147.

_____

_____

_____

2 Why should every house have a smoke alarm?

Hint
See page 148.

_____

_____

_____

3 What changes Randy's mind about fire safety?

Hint
See pages 149 and 150.

_____

_____

_____

Be a Reading Detective!

Look back at "Officer Buckle and Gloria."

Think about the questions. Look for clues.

"Officer Buckle and Gloria"
Student Book pp. 507–529

1 **Who** are the characters?

2 **How** does Gloria help Officer Buckle?

Write your answer.

1 **Who** are the characters?

_____

_____

_____

_____

_____

Talk about question 2. Tell about the clues you found.

2 **How** does Gloria help Officer Buckle?

Helping People

1 Helping a friend can be fun. You won't be **disappointed** if you help a friend.

Why won't you be <u>disappointed</u> if you work hard at school?

_____

_____

2 I like to help people. I helped my brother learn to ride a bike. I was happy when he learned. He was, too. We both **chuckled**.

What is another word for <u>chuckled</u>?

_____

3 One day, I saw a girl at school. She was **staring** at the room numbers. I asked her if she needed help. She did. I showed her the right room.

Tell about a time you were <u>staring</u> at something unusual.

_____

_____

_____

4 Last Monday, I **received** a box. I looked at the name. The box was sent to the wrong house! I took it to Mr. Tam's house. He thanked me.

Tell about a time you <u>received</u> something in the mail.

_____

_____

_____

Kate's Helping Day

by Margaret Maugenest

Kate woke up early. It was a special day. She planned to help people.

Kate had promised to help her mom first. Kate was **staring** into space when her mom called her.

Stop **Think** **Write**

VOCABULARY

A word that has the same meaning as <u>staring</u> is _____

_____.

154

Kate's mom was wearing a hat and gloves. "Are you really going to help me?" asked Mom.

"Sure," said Kate. "May I wear a hat and gloves, too?"

"Yes," said Mom.

Stop | **Think** | **Write**

UNDERSTANDING CHARACTERS

Kate wants to wear a hat and

_____

Kate helped out in the garden. Mom told her all about plants. Kate had fun. "We've worked a long time. We're done, Kate," said Mom. "Who will you help next?"

Stop | Think | Write

STORY STRUCTURE

Kate helps her mom. She learns about

_____.

"I'm helping my friend Carol," said Kate. "We're going to paint her room."

Kate put on some old clothes. Then she walked to Carol's home.

Kate hoped she'd like painting. It was hard but fun. She was not **disappointed**.

Stop **Think** **Write**

SEQUENCE OF EVENTS

Kate puts on old clothes. What does she do next?

_____

_____

_____

157

The friends liked painting the walls.
Paint splashed on their old clothes.
They looked in a mirror. They
chuckled about the paint spills.

Stop Think Write

VOCABULARY

Kate and Carol _____ about
the paint on their clothes.

Next, Kate helped her friend Ramón.
She went to his house. They washed his
dad's car.

It was hard work. It was worth it.
Ramón's dad paid them. Each of them
received a few dollars.

Stop **Think** **Write**

STORY STRUCTURE

Kate is at _____ house.

159

That night, Kate was tired but happy.
She thought about the day.

She had learned about plants.

She had made a room pretty. She had earned money.

Kate smiled. She liked helping out.

Stop **Think** **Write**

STORY STRUCTURE

At the end of the story, Kate feels tired and

_____

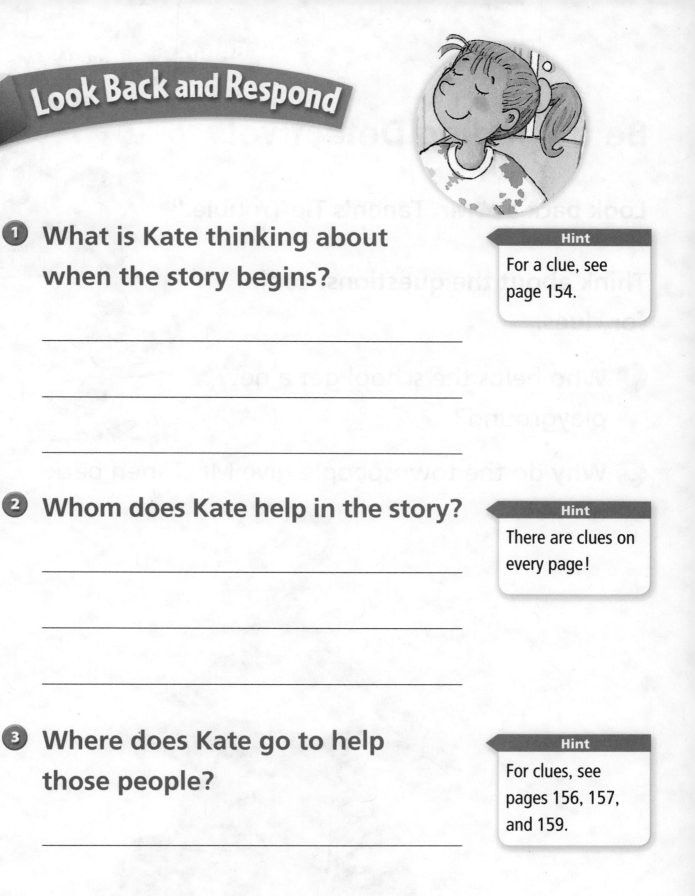

Look Back and Respond

1 **What is Kate thinking about when the story begins?**

Hint

For a clue, see page 154.

_____

_____

_____

2 **Whom does Kate help in the story?**

Hint

There are clues on every page!

_____

_____

_____

3 **Where does Kate go to help those people?**

Hint

For clues, see pages 156, 157, and 159.

_____

_____

_____

Return to

"Mr. Tanen's Tie Trouble"
Student Book pp. 15–35

Be a Reading Detective!

Look back at "Mr. Tanen's Tie Trouble."

Think about the questions. Look for clues.

1 **Who** helps the school get a new playground?

2 **Why** do the townspeople give Mr. Tanen back his ties?

Write your answer. Use details and examples from the story.

1 **Who** helps the school get a new playground?

_____

_____

_____

_____

Talk about question 2. Tell about the clues you found.

2 **Why** do the townspeople give Mr. Tanen back his ties?

A Good Teacher

Check the answer.

1 It was the _____ day of first grade. Lisa was sad. Now she had to say goodbye to Mr. Lee.

☐ **busy** ☐ **final** ☐ **deepest**

2 She thought about her year at school. Math was hard. Mr. Lee spent _____ time with her. He wanted to make sure she learned.

☐ **extra** ☐ **rotten** ☐ **plain**

3 It worked! Lisa did a fine job in math. She got a good test score. Mr. Lee _____ for her. She would miss Mr. Lee.

☐ **hurried** ☐ **received** ☐ **cheered**

4 What is the <u>final</u> thing you do before going to bed?

_____

_____

_____

5 Tell about a time you <u>hurried</u> somewhere.

_____

_____

_____

True Heroes

by Karen Bischoff

Josh loved baseball. The Stars were his favorite team. The player Rick Callan was his hero. Josh had never been to a game. He had seen games only on TV.

Stop | **Think** | **Write**

Josh's favorite baseball team is

_____ .

One day, Josh's dad came home smiling. "My boss had **extra** tickets to the game," he said. "He gave them to me." "Wow!" shouted Josh. He was happy.

Stop | **Think** | **Write**

SEQUENCE OF EVENTS

Josh's dad shows Josh tickets to the game. Then

Josh is _____.

165

The game was great. Josh could see all the players. He **cheered** a lot.

He loved to watch Rick Callan. He played like a hero. He hit a home run. The **final** score was 7 to 4. The Stars won.

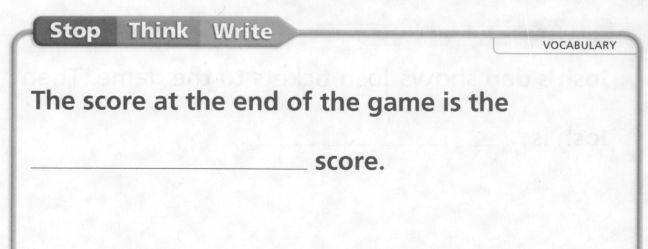

VOCABULARY

The score at the end of the game is the

_____ score.

On the way to the car, Josh stopped. He saw Rick Callan! Josh **hurried** over to him. "Will you sign my program?" he asked.

"Sorry. I'm in a rush," Rick Callan said. He kept walking.

Stop **Think** **Write**

VOCABULARY

Josh _____ over to Rick Callan because he did not want to miss him.

Josh was upset. Rick Callan had not
been nice to him. Josh said, "I thought
he was a hero. I was wrong."

"Never mind," Dad said. "I can take
you to a real hero."

Stop Think Write

SEQUENCE OF EVENTS

After meeting Rick Callan, Josh is

_____.

168

Josh's dad took him to a house. "Josh, this is Mrs. Evans. I had a secret. She helped me with it," Dad said.

"What was the secret?" Josh asked.

"I couldn't read," said Dad.

Stop Think Write

Josh meets Mrs. Evans _____
the game.

"Mrs. Evans taught me to read," Dad said. "She's my hero. A hero teaches you something."

"Your dad is my hero," said Mrs. Evans. "He worked hard to learn."

Josh smiled. "I have two new heroes now," he said.

Stop **Think** **Write**

Josh's dad thinks Mrs. Evans is a

_____.

Look Back and Respond

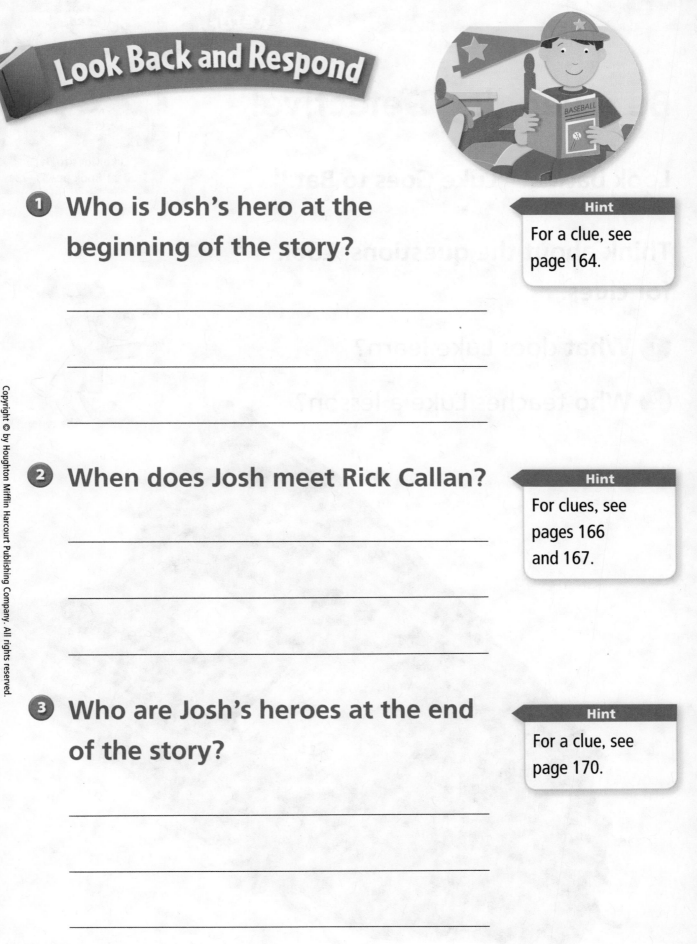

1 Who is Josh's hero at the beginning of the story?

Hint
For a clue, see page 164.

_____

_____

_____

2 When does Josh meet Rick Callan?

Hint
For clues, see pages 166 and 167.

_____

_____

_____

3 Who are Josh's heroes at the end of the story?

Hint
For a clue, see page 170.

_____

_____

_____

Return to

"Luke Goes to Bat"
Student Book pp. 53–73

Be a Reading Detective!

Look back at "Luke Goes to Bat."

Think about the questions. Look for clues.

1. **What** does Luke learn?

2. **Who** teaches Luke a lesson?

Write your answer. Use details and examples from the story.

1 **What** does Luke learn?

_____

_____

_____

_____

_____

Talk about question 2. Tell about the clues you found.

2 **Who** teaches Luke a lesson?

How Writers Work

express

pretend

prize

taught

1 A writer uses words. The words explain how the writer feels. Words **express** the writer's feelings.

Do you write about your feelings? Name a feeling you might want to <u>express</u>.

_____

2 Most writers say that they like to read. They say that reading books **taught** them to write.

Name something that books have <u>taught</u> you.

_____

_____

_____

3 Writers use their imaginations. They may **pretend** they have done something. They may write about an event as if it really happened.

Do you ever <u>pretend</u> to be in a place that isn't real? Explain.

_____

_____

_____

4 Sometimes a very good book wins a **prize**.

Think of the books you like. What book would you give a <u>prize</u> to?

_____

_____

_____

Pat Mora
by Jean Casella

Pat Mora grew up in Texas.
She spoke two languages.
Pat spoke English. She spoke
Spanish, too.

Stop **Think** **Write**

MAIN IDEAS AND DETAILS

Pat spoke English and _____.

174

Pat's grandparents grew up in Mexico. Pat spoke Spanish with them.

Pat's aunt grew up in Mexico, too. She told stories about growing up there. She told some stories in English. She told some in Spanish. Pat loved her aunt's stories.

Stop | **Think** | **Write**

CAUSE AND EFFECT

Why did Pat's aunt speak Spanish?

_____

_____

_____

175

Pat loved to read. She read about places far away. She liked to **pretend** she was there.

There were always books in Pat's house. Her mother would drive her to the library, too.

Stop Think Write

Pat liked to _____ she was in a faraway place.

At school, all the lessons were in English. So Pat spoke English at school. She also spoke it at home.

When Pat grew up, she became a teacher. She **taught** kids to read and write.

Stop | **Think** | **Write**

VOCABULARY

Name the things Pat <u>taught</u> her students.

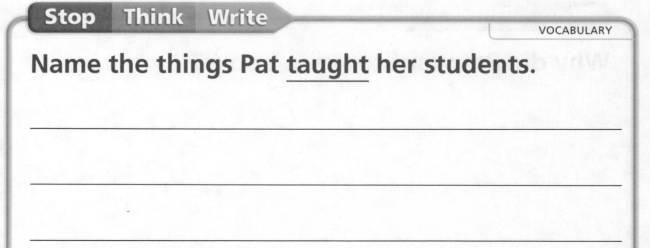

_____

_____

_____

Pat had a lot of ideas. She wanted to write books. She wanted to **express** her ideas in words.

Pat wanted to write about growing up in Texas. She wanted to write about speaking two languages.

Stop **Think** **Write**

UNDERSTANDING CHARACTERS

Why did Pat want to write books?

_____

_____

_____

Pat started to write books. Her books won a **prize**. Then she wrote more books.

Pat wrote about families like hers. She told stories, just like her aunt did.

Stop | Think | Write

UNDERSTANDING CHARACTERS

Why was Pat's aunt important to her?

_____

_____

_____

Some of Pat's books are in English. Some of her books are in Spanish.

Some of her books have English words and Spanish words. They use two languages—just like Pat!

Stop   Think   Write

What is unusual about some of Pat's books?

_____

_____

_____

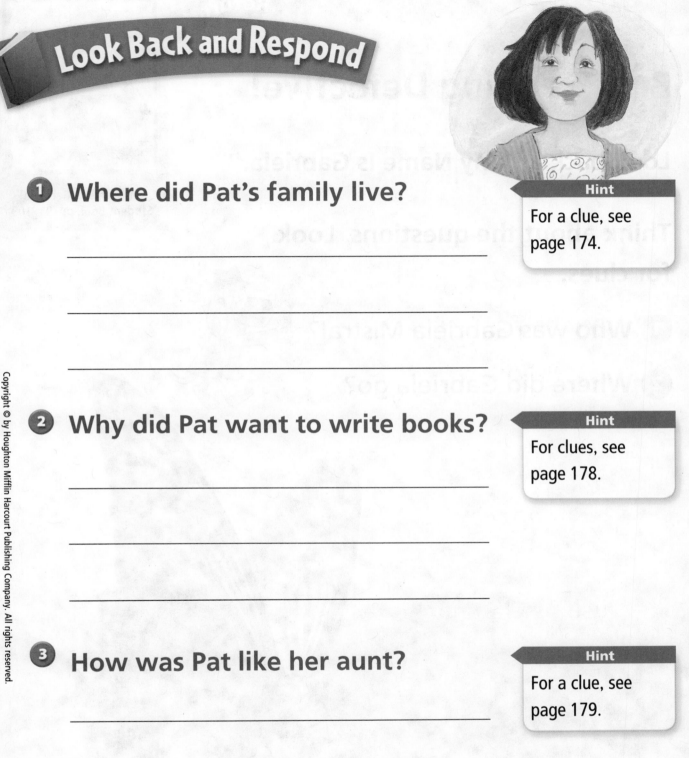

Look Back and Respond

1 **Where did Pat's family live?**

Hint

For a clue, see page 174.

_____

_____

_____

2 **Why did Pat want to write books?**

Hint

For clues, see page 178.

_____

_____

_____

3 **How was Pat like her aunt?**

Hint

For a clue, see page 179.

_____

_____

_____

Be a Reading Detective!

Look back at "My Name Is Gabriela."

"My Name Is Gabriela"
Student Book pp. 91–109

Think about the questions. Look for clues.

1 **Who** was Gabriela Mistral?

2 **Where** did Gabriela go?

Write your answer. Use details and examples from the selection.

1 **Who** was Gabriela Mistral?

_____

_____

_____

_____

_____

_____

Talk about question 2. Tell about the clues you found.

2 **Where** did Gabriela go?

A Wrong Turn

1 My sister and I had **trouble** finding our way. We took a wrong turn. We got lost.

Name something that you have <u>trouble</u> doing.

_____

_____

_____

2 We **failed** to get home. Our parents would be worried.

What was the last thing you <u>failed</u> to do?

_____

_____

_____

3 I said we should stop. We should ask for directions. My sister **agreed**.

What is something that you and your friends _agreed_ on last week?

_____

_____

_____

4 A girl helped us. She told us how to get home. She was very **polite**.

Describe a way that you are _polite_.

_____

_____

_____

The Big City

by John Berry

Sam looked out the window. Texas was fading away. His dad was reading a paper. His mom was reading a book.

Sam's family was moving to New York City. Sam was sad. He missed Texas already.

Stop **Think** **Write**

TEXT AND GRAPHIC FEATURES

Who is the author of this story?

_____

_____

_____

184

At last the plane landed. New York City looked very tall. Sam stared. He did not know this city. He did not have friends here. He might have **trouble** feeling at home.

| Stop | Think | Write |

UNDERSTANDING CHARACTERS

Sam doesn't know the city. He doesn't have any

_____ in New York.

They went to their new home. Sam couldn't sleep that night. He heard horns. He heard sirens. His mom and dad were awake, too.

"What shall we do tomorrow?" said his mom. "Let's plan."

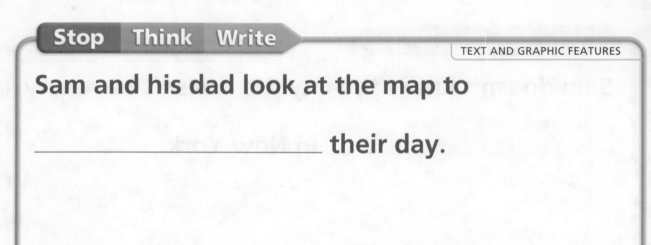

TEXT AND GRAPHIC FEATURES

Sam and his dad look at the map to

_____ their day.

The next day, they got on the subway. Sam's dad wanted to go to a hardware store. They **failed** to get there. They were on the wrong subway. "Next stop, Yankee Stadium," said a voice.

"The baseball stadium?" said Sam. "Wow!"

Stop **Think** **Write**

VOCABULARY

The family took the wrong subway. They

_____ to get to the store.

Sam's mom and dad looked at him.
They looked at each other. They smiled.

"Shall we go to the game?" asked
his mom.

"Yes!" said Sam.

His dad **agreed**. They bought tickets.
It was a great game. It was a great day.

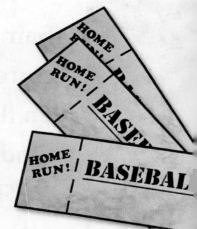

| Stop | Think | Write |

VOCABULARY

Sam and his parents <u>agreed</u>. They would go to

the _____.

They took a subway the next day, too. Sam's mom wanted to shop for curtains. They got on the wrong subway again.

They looked at the map. A **polite** man helped. "Are you new here?" he said. "You're near a good museum. You should go there."

Stop | Think | Write

MAIN IDEAS AND DETAILS

The family is near a _____.

Sam and his family found the museum. They saw a blue whale. They saw rocks and gems. They saw bugs and snakes.

They walked into a big room. Sam stared. Dinosaurs! "Wow," said Sam. "New York isn't so bad after all!"

TEXT AND GRAPHIC FEATURES

What is the family looking at?

_____

_____

_____

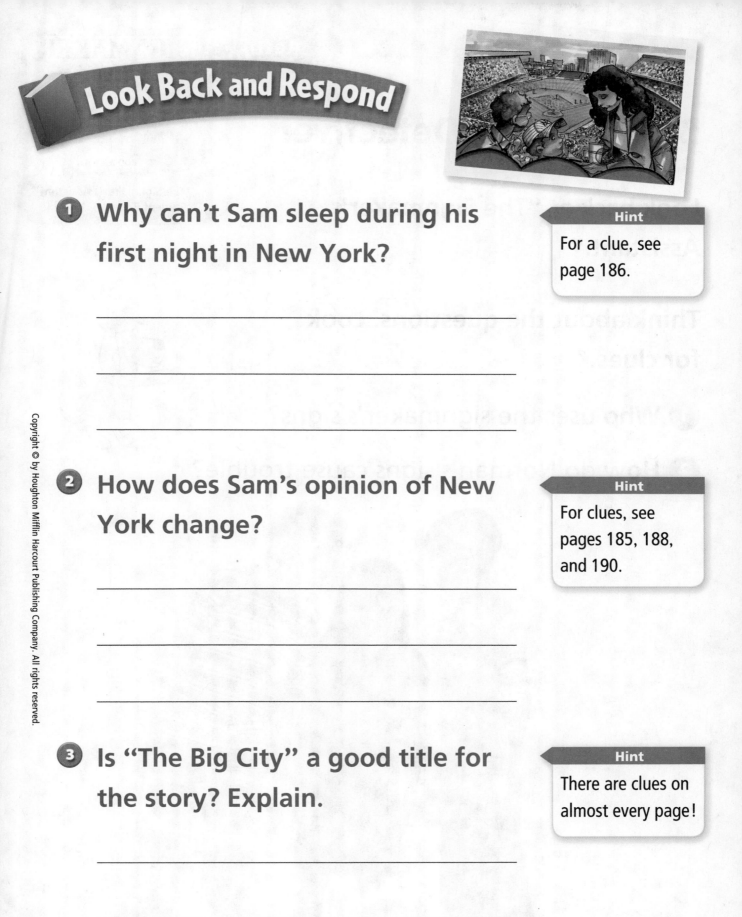

Look Back and Respond

1 Why can't Sam sleep during his first night in New York?

Hint
For a clue, see page 186.

_____

_____

_____

2 How does Sam's opinion of New York change?

Hint
For clues, see pages 185, 188, and 190.

_____

_____

_____

3 Is "The Big City" a good title for the story? Explain.

Hint
There are clues on almost every page!

_____

_____

_____

Be a Reading Detective!

Return to

THE SIGNMAKER's ASSISTANT

TEDD ARNOLD

"The Signmaker's Assistant"
Student Book pp. 127–149

Look back at "The Signmaker's Assistant."

Think about the questions. Look for clues.

1 **Who** uses the signmaker's signs?

2 **How** do Norman's signs cause trouble?

Write your answer. Use details and examples from the selection.

1 **Who** uses the signmaker's signs?

_____

_____

_____

_____

_____

Talk about question 2. Tell about the clues you found.

2 **How** do Norman's signs cause trouble?

STOP

gazing

sore

sprang

studied

A Maple Tree

1 A girl was _____ at a tree. She thought it was pretty.

2 She knew it was a maple tree. She _____ trees in class. She knew the different types.

3 A gust of wind blew leaves off the

tree. She _____ up
and grabbed a rake.

4 Raking leaves was hard work. It

made her _____.
Her arms hurt.

Write the vocabulary word that best completes the synonym web.

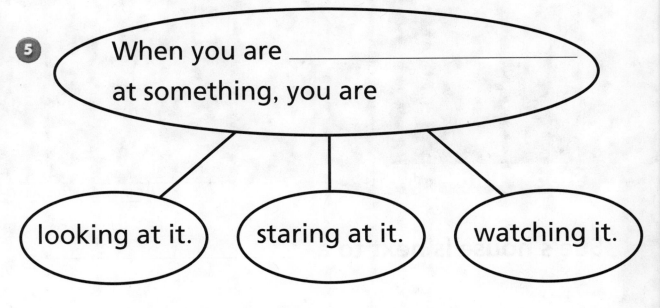

5 When you are _____ at something, you are

looking at it.   staring at it.   watching it.

Sue and the Tired Wolf

by John Berry

Sue lived in a blue house with her mom and dad. The house had a big yard. It was next to a forest.

Sue **studied** music. She played songs on her flute every day.

Stop | **Think** | **Write**

MAIN IDEAS AND DETAILS

Sue's house is next to a _____.

One day, Sue's mom and dad wanted some quiet. "Too much noise!" they said.

"I will go outside, then," said Sue. Her mom told her to play in the yard. She should not go in the woods. Sue agreed.

She sat in a leaf pile. She played her flute loudly.

Stop | **Think** | **Write**

STORY STRUCTURE

Sue's mom and dad want less

_____.

Sue got bored. She wanted to explore the woods. She told herself she would go for just a bit. She walked into the forest.

The trees were tall. The forest was dark. Sue kept playing her flute. She liked the sound of her flute in the forest.

Stop | **Think** | **Write**

CAUSE AND EFFECT

Why does Sue walk into the forest?

_____

_____

_____

All of a sudden, Sue stopped playing. A wolf was sitting on a rock. He was **gazing** at her.

"You surprised me!" Sue said. She was scared. She tried to smile.

"I like the sound of your flute. I think this forest is too quiet," said the wolf.

Stop | Think | Write

UNDERSTANDING CHARACTERS

The wolf likes Sue's music. He thinks the

forest is too _____.

197

The wolf was tired and **sore**. He said, "I have been hunting all day. I want to rest and listen to music."

Sue played her flute. The wolf grew sleepy. His eyelids closed as Sue played.

Stop Think Write

The wolf has been hunting all day. His muscles hurt. He is _____.

Sue began to run away, but the wolf woke up. He **sprang** off the rock. "Why did you stop?" he asked.

"I have to get home," said Sue.

"You can't go! Play more!"

Stop **Think** **Write**

The wolf woke up. Then he

_____ off the rock.

Sue blew a new tune. The wolf grew sleepy again. He started to snore.

Sue walked a few steps. Then she played again. The wolf snored louder. The trick seemed to work!

She used the trick a few more times. At last she was home! Now she knew why she had to stay out of the woods.

Stop   Think   Write

STORY STRUCTURE

How does Sue get away from the wolf?

200

Look Back and Respond

1 Sue's yard is safe to play in.
What is the forest like?

Hint

For clues, see pages 196 and 197.

_____

_____

_____

2 What does the wolf think of Sue's music?

Hint

For a clue, see page 197.

_____

_____

_____

3 Do you think Sue will go back to the forest?

Hint

For a clue, see page 200.

_____

_____

Return to

"Dex: The Heart of a Hero"
Student Book pp. 167–189

Be a Reading Detective!

Look back at "Dex: The Heart of a Hero."

Think about the questions. Look for clues.

1 **How** does Cleevis the cat change?

2 **What** makes Dex a hero?

THE AMAZING
MEGATUFF
ANOTHER KICKIN' ISSUE!

MEGA COMICS

M
28
APRIL
$2.95

Write your answer. Use details and examples from the selection.

1 How does Cleevis the cat change?

_____

_____

_____

_____

_____

Talk about question 2. Tell about the clues you found.

2 What makes Dex a hero?

Turtles

All turtles have shells. A turtle has a shell on the top. It has a shell on the bottom. The shells get **slippery** when they are wet.

A turtle needs its shell. The shell keeps the turtle safe. **Otherwise**, the turtle might get eaten. It has enemies!

Many turtles live in water. They have **webbed** feet. Water turtles sleep all winter. They sleep at the bottom of ponds and lakes. Then the spring comes. The water gets warm. **Finally**, the turtles wake up.

1 At the end of winter, the turtles

_____ wake up.

2 A turtle's shell gets

_____ when it is wet.

3 A turtle's shell keeps it safe.
The turtle might be eaten,

_____ .

4 Name other animals that

have <u>webbed</u> feet.

_____

_____

_____

Joe and Trig
and the
Baby
Turtles

by Karen Bischoff

A turtle came out of a lake. She found some sand and made a nest with her **webbed** feet. Then she laid her eggs. The turtle pushed sand on top of her eggs. When her work was **finally** done, she went back to the lake.

Stop Think Write

The turtle has feet that are _____.

Many days passed. The eggs cracked. One baby turtle was fast. It got out of its shell first. It pushed its way out of the nest. It needed to get to the water. It was not safe on the ground. Birds like to eat baby turtles.

Stop **Think** **Write**

CAUSE AND EFFECT

Why does the turtle need to get to the water?

Close by, Joe was fishing. His Uncle Rob brought him to the lake. Joe had his dog, Trig.

Trig was sniffing around the edge of the lake. Trig barked. Joe went over to Trig.

CONCLUSIONS

What makes Joe go to see Trig?

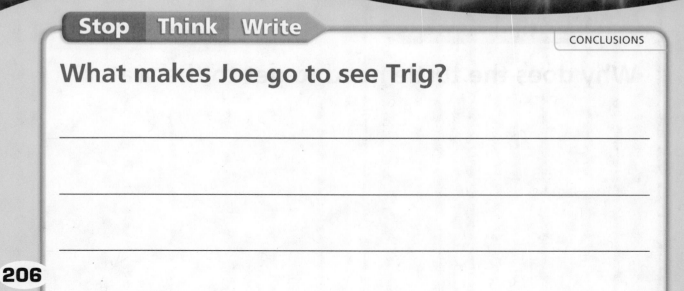

Trig had found the baby turtle. It was stuck in some mud.

"Good job, Trig!" said Joe.

Joe picked up the turtle. He put it in a pool of water near the lake. The turtle splashed up and down in the fresh water.

Stop | **Think** | **Write**

CAUSE AND EFFECT

Why does Joe pick up the baby turtle?

_____

_____

_____

Joe looked around. "Are there more turtles?" he asked Trig. "We may need to help them, too."

Trig sniffed the ground and tracked the baby turtle's path. Joe followed. They headed for the turtles' nest.

Stop   Think   Write

MAIN IDEAS AND DETAILS

Trig sniffed the path that led to the turtles'

_____

Uncle Rob looked for Joe and Trig. "Where are you?" he called.

"We're over here," said Joe. "We're watching turtles."

Uncle Rob found them by the nest. The turtles were working hard. They had to dig their way out of the slippery sand.

Stop **Think** **Write**

VOCABULARY

It was hard for the turtles to get out of the nest because it was _____.

Joe and Uncle Rob watched the turtles go to the lake.

"They will be safe now," said Joe.

"It's good that you found that first turtle," said Uncle Rob. "Otherwise, they all might have been in trouble."

"Trig found it!" said Joe.

Stop | Think | Write

MAIN IDEAS AND DETAILS

Who found the first baby turtle?

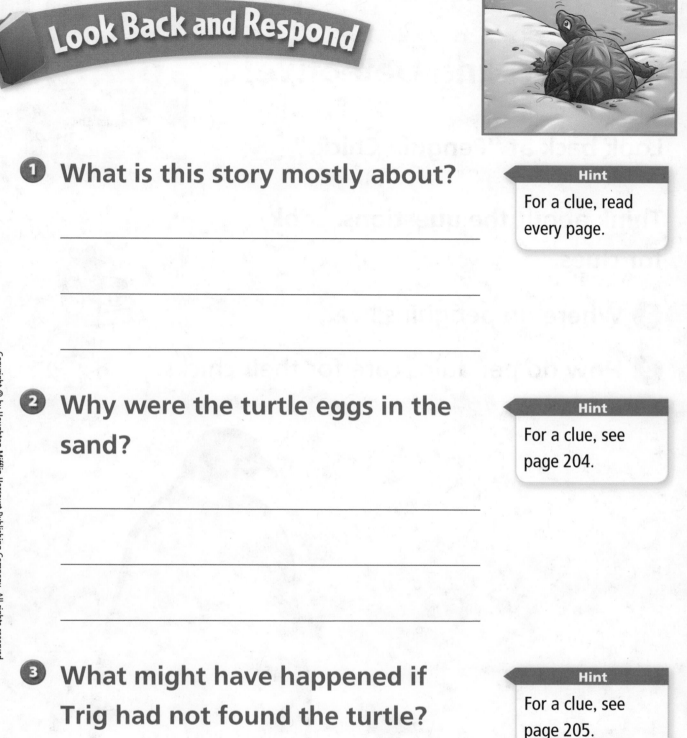

Look Back and Respond

1 **What is this story mostly about?**

Hint

For a clue, read every page.

_____

_____

_____

2 **Why were the turtle eggs in the sand?**

Hint

For a clue, see page 204.

_____

_____

_____

3 **What might have happened if Trig had not found the turtle?**

Hint

For a clue, see page 205.

_____

_____

_____

Return to

Penguin Chick

"Penguin Chick"
Student Book pp. 211–227

Be a Reading Detective!

Look back at "Penguin Chick."

**Think about the questions. Look
for clues.**

1 **Where** do penguins live?

2 **How** do penguins care for their chicks?

Write your answer. Use details and examples from the selection.

1 **Where** do penguins live?

_____

_____

_____

_____

_____

_____

Talk about question 2. Tell about the clues you found.

2 **How** do penguins care for their chicks?

New Neighbors

1 Dad helped people next door. He lugged big boxes. He was breathing **heavily**.

Why does Dad breathe <u>heavily</u> when he carries the boxes?

_____

_____

_____

2 Dad spoke **seriously** to me. He asked me to go next door. He wanted me to introduce myself.

What do you do <u>seriously</u>?

_____

_____

_____

3 I had chores to do. I was **planning** to take out the trash. Dad said it could wait.

What are you planning to do after school today?

_____

_____

_____

4 I rang my new neighbor's bell. A boy my age **answered**. Now I have a new friend!

Have you answered the phone recently? Who was calling?

_____

_____

_____

Flood on River Road

by Shirley Granahan

It rained all day. It rained all night.

It rained **heavily** for days.

"I am sick of rain," said Jody.

"Me, too," I said. "At least we're

warm and dry."

Stop | Think | Write

VOCABULARY

A lot of rain falls. It falls _____

for days.

214

We looked down the hill. Water covered River Road. It spilled into Mr. Lee's house.

"This is a flood!" Mom said **seriously.** "We must help Mr. Lee!"

Stop **Think** **Write**

UNDERSTANDING CHARACTERS

Mom wants to help _____.

Mr. Lee stayed at our house. He kept **planning** to go home. He had to wait until the water went down. At last, it did.

Mr. Lee went to his house. His things were wet and muddy. Neighbors gave him some new things to use.

STORY STRUCTURE

What is Mr. Lee's house like after the flood?

_____

_____

_____

"Thank you!" he said. He was still worried. What if the water came back?

"Can we have a party to make Mr. Lee happy again?" I asked Mom.

"Good idea!" she **answered**.

Stop | Think | Write

What word could you use instead of <u>answered</u>?

_____

At the party, Jody and I sang a silly song. I barked like a dog.

There was a knock at the door. A man gave Mr. Lee a letter. He read it and smiled.

UNDERSTANDING CHARACTERS

Mr. Lee is _____ when he reads

the letter.

218

Mr. Lee showed us the letter. "I have been offered a new home," he said. "It is up on a hill. I will not have to worry about floods!"

Stop **Think** **Write**

UNDERSTANDING CHARACTERS

How does Mr. Lee feel about his new home?

_____

_____

_____

_____

We were glad. The house was not far away. Mr. Lee would still be our neighbor!

"Come visit me," he said. "You, too, silly dog. You helped me to laugh!"

Stop **Think** **Write**

People are glad that Mr. Lee will still be their

_____.

Look Back and Respond

1 **Is Mom a good neighbor? Explain.**

Hint

For a clue, see page 215.

_____

_____

_____

2 **How do Mr. Lee's neighbors help him after the flood?**

Hint

For clues, see pages 216 and 217.

_____

_____

_____

3 **How do you think Mr. Lee feels about his neighbors?**

Hint

For clues, see pages 217 and 220.

_____

_____

_____

Return to

The Stories Julian Tells

Ann Cameron

"Gloria Who Might Be
My Best Friend"
Student Book pp. 245–261

Be a Reading Detective!

Look back at "Gloria Who Might Be My Best Friend."

Think about the questions. Look for clues.

1 **What** do Julian and Gloria do together?

2 **How** does Julian feel about Gloria?

Write your answer. Use details and examples from the story.

1 **What** do Julian and Gloria do together?

_____

_____

_____

_____

_____

Talk about question 2. Tell about the clues you found.

2 **How** does Julian feel about Gloria?

duplicated

dye

strands

yarn

Making Things

1 Yolanda wants to make mittens. She needs to get **yarn** first.

Name something else you can knit with <u>yarn</u>.

_____

_____

_____

2 Tim has a white shirt. He soaks it in red **dye**. Now he has a red shirt.

You soaked a white shirt in blue <u>dye</u>. What color is the shirt now?

_____

_____

_____

3 Javier has **strands** of yarn. They are red, blue, and white. He braids the yarn. He makes a bracelet.

You want to make a friendship bracelet from <u>strands</u> of yarn. Which colors would you pick?

_____

_____

_____

4 Nick made a drawing. Nora wants to make one like it. She copies the drawing. Hers looks just the same! She **duplicated** his drawing.

What have you <u>duplicated</u>?

_____

_____

_____

I Made It Myself

by Margaret Maugenest

My grandma and I take a walk. We pass a shop window. I point to a red scarf.

"That's pretty," I say.

"You can knit a scarf like this," says Ama. "I'll show you how, Rosie."

"Really?" I ask.

Stop **Think** **Write**

CONCLUSIONS

Rosie likes a red

_____.

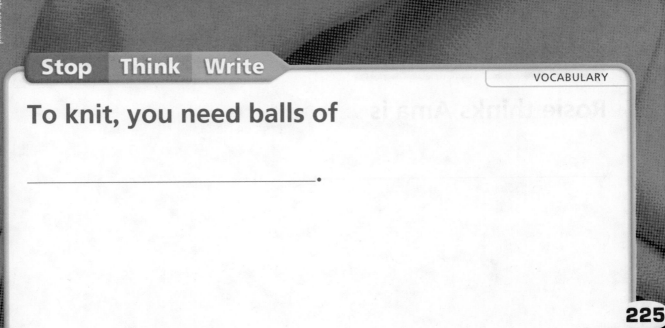

We go to Ama's house. Ama gets a box. Inside are balls of white **yarn**.

"You can use this to make a scarf," she says.

"This yarn is white," I say. "I want a red scarf."

Stop | **Think** | **Write**

VOCABULARY

To knit, you need balls of

_____.

"I can make it red," says Ama. "I know how. I'll soak it in red **dye**."

"You're so smart. You can do anything!" I say. I give Ama a big hug.

I go to Ama's house the next day. The wool is red.

Stop **Think** **Write**

UNDERSTANDING CHARACTERS

Rosie thinks Ama is

_____.

"Let's knit," Ama says.

She shows me how to hold the knitting needles. "Bring the yarn under first. Then bring it over the needle," she says.

Stop **Think** **Write**

MAIN IDEAS AND DETAILS

Ama shows Rosie how to

_____.

I make my first stitch.
I make another stitch.
I finish my first row.
Then I knit another row.

"I don't see much scarf yet," I say.

"It takes time," says Ama.

"It sure does!" I say.

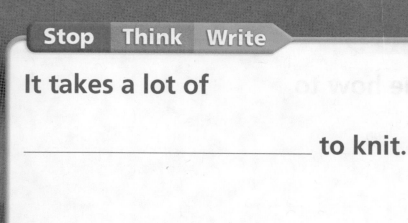

Stop | **Think** | **Write**

It takes a lot of

_____ to knit.

I knit every day. My cat Ruby likes to watch. I cut some **strands** of yarn. She plays with them.

My scarf starts to get long.

I keep knitting. My scarf is getting longer!

Stop | **Think** | **Write**

CONCLUSIONS

How can you tell Rosie likes to knit?

_____

_____

_____

I knit for many weeks.

At last, my scarf is done. Ama helps me finish it. I put it around my neck.

"Thank you. It is beautiful," I say.

"I'm proud of you," says Ama. "You **duplicated** the scarf! You're a real knitter!"

VOCABULARY

Rosie is a real knitter. She

_____ the red scarf she saw.

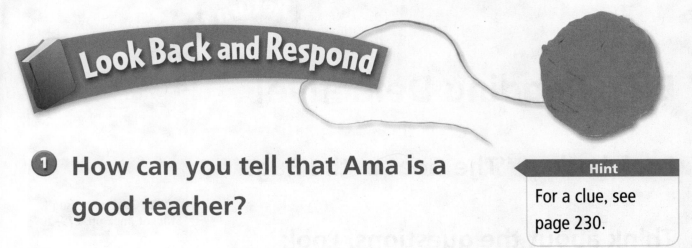

Look Back and Respond

1 How can you tell that Ama is a good teacher?

Hint
For a clue, see page 230.

_____

_____

_____

2 Does it take Rosie a long time to knit her scarf? How do you know?

Hint
For clues, see pages 228, 229, and 230.

_____

_____

_____

3 How can you tell that Rosie and Ama get along well?

Hint
Clues are on almost every page!

_____

_____

_____

Return to

THE GOAT
IN THE RUG

As told to Charles L. Blood & Martin Link

BY GERALDINE

Illustrated by
Nancy Winslow Parker

"The Goat in the Rug"
Student Book pp. 279–297

Be a Reading Detective!

Look back at "The Goat in the Rug."

Think about the questions. Look for clues.

1 Who is Geraldine?

2 What is the first step to making the rug?

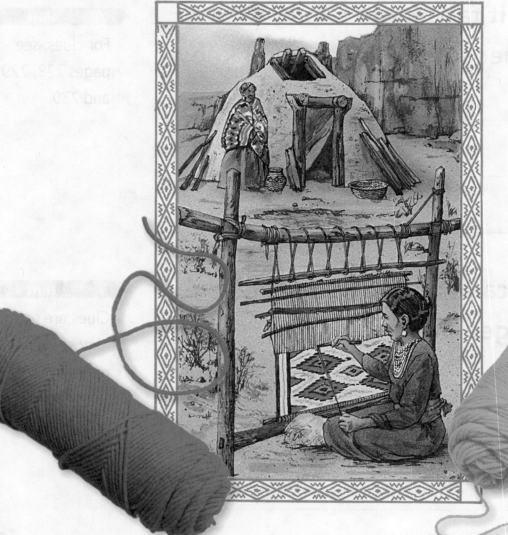

Write your answer. Use details and examples from the selection.

1 **Who** is Geraldine?

_____

_____

_____

_____

Talk about question 2. Tell about the clues you found.

2 **What** is the first step to making the rug?

By the Stream

I took my little paper boat
And put it in the **stream**.
The boat was bobbing up and down.
I fell into a dream.

I sailed the mighty Rio Grande.
For Big Bend, I was bound.
The rushing water got quite **swift**.
The boat was **flung** around.

I dreamed it ran into a rock
And sank into the deep.
But all was well, and so I fell
Back **peacefully** to sleep.

1 The boat was _____ this way and that in the water.

2 I put my paper boat into the

_____.

3 The rushing water became very

_____.

4 Describe a place where you can sit peacefully.

_____

_____

_____

The Contest

by Mia Lewis

Sun and Wind were talking.

"I'm stronger than you," said Wind. "I can blow a ship across the sea. I can bend a tree to the ground."

"I'm stronger!" said Sun. "I light the day. I can dry up that **stream!**"

Stop	Think	Write

VOCABULARY

If you walk in a _____, your feet will get wet.

Sun saw a man on the road.

"That man is wearing a coat," said Sun. "We will have a contest. If you can make the man take off his coat, you are stronger. If I can make him take it off, I am stronger. You go first!"

Stop | **Think** | **Write**

CAUSE AND EFFECT

Why does Sun want to have a contest?

_____

_____

_____

235

Wind agreed. He wasted no time. He blew a **swift** breeze at the man. The traveler did not notice.

Wind blew a stronger gust. The man held onto his hat. He kept walking.

Stop | Think | Write

CAUSE AND EFFECT

Why does Wind blow a strong gust at the man?

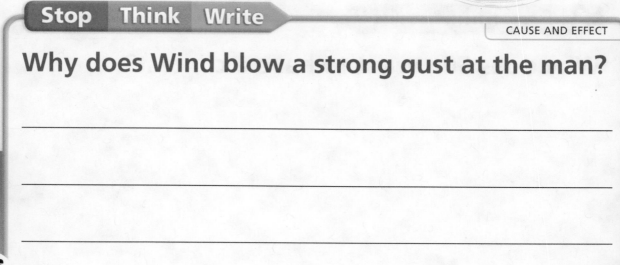

Now Wind blew a real storm! The trees shook! Leaves were **flung** into the air.

Wind blew as hard as he could. The man only pulled his coat more tightly around himself.

Stop | Think | Write

VOCABULARY

The strong wind _____ the leaves into the air.

At last Wind gave up. "You try," he said to Sun. "Good luck!"

Sun smiled. He shone a little ray. The man kept on walking.

"You see," said Wind. "Neither of us can get him to take off his coat."

Stop | Think | Write

INFER AND PREDICT

Why do you think Sun smiles?

_____

_____

_____

Sun was not finished. He shone another ray on the man. He beat down hot and steady.

The man began to sweat. He took off his hat. He opened his coat. After a while, he took his coat all the way off.

Stop **Think** **Write**

CAUSE AND EFFECT

Why does the man take off his coat ?

_____

_____

_____

Wind clapped. Sun bowed. The man walked **peacefully** down the road in his T-shirt.

The story has a moral. Persuade gently. It works better than force.

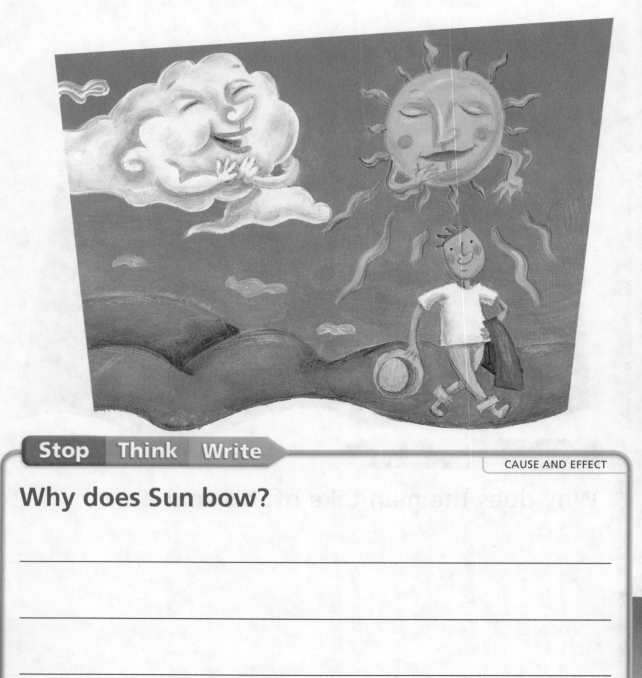

Stop **Think** **Write**

CAUSE AND EFFECT

Why does Sun bow?

_____

_____

_____

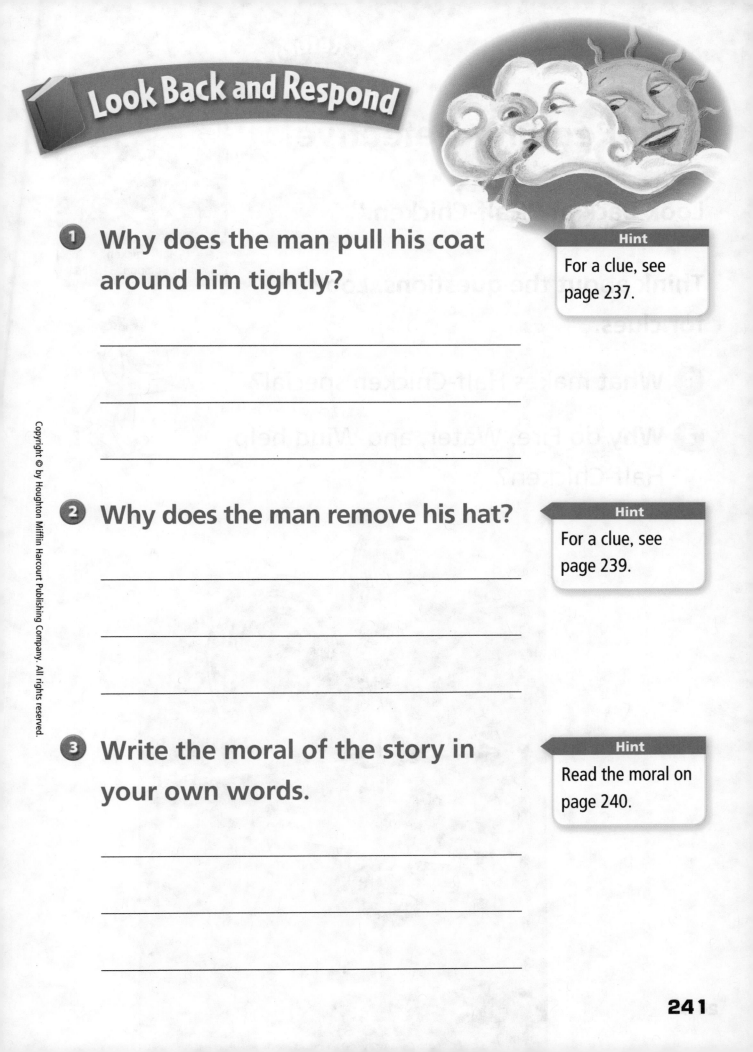

Look Back and Respond

1 **Why does the man pull his coat around him tightly?**

Hint
For a clue, see page 237.

_____

_____

_____

2 **Why does the man remove his hat?**

Hint
For a clue, see page 239.

_____

_____

_____

3 **Write the moral of the story in your own words.**

Hint
Read the moral on page 240.

_____

_____

_____

"Half-Chicken"
Student Book pp. 315–331

Be a Reading Detective!

Look back at "Half-Chicken."

Think about the questions. Look
for clues.

1 **What** makes Half-Chicken special?

2 **Why** do Fire, Water, and Wind help
Half-Chicken?

Write your answer. Use details and examples from the story.

1 **What** makes Half-Chicken special?

_____

_____

_____

_____

_____

Talk about question 2. Tell about the clues you found.

2 **Why** do Fire, Water, and Wind help Half-Chicken?

grain

nutrition

soak

tasty

A Grain of Wheat

1 Each **grain** of wheat is covered with a hard outer layer. This layer is called the bran.

What word or phrase could you use instead of <u>grain</u>?

_____

2 There is a lot of **nutrition** in wheat bran. That's why whole grain flour is so good for you.

List two other foods that have good <u>nutrition</u>.

_____

_____

3 To sprout a grain of wheat, **soak** it in water overnight. It will begin to grow.

What happens if you <u>soak</u> a piece of paper?

_____

_____

_____

4 You can cook with sprouted wheat. Sprouted wheat bread is very **tasty**.

Write a word that means the same as <u>tasty</u>.

_____

Growing Sprouts

by Mia Lewis

Do you eat sprouts? Maybe you eat them on sandwiches. Maybe you eat them in salads. They are used in cooked food, too.

Stop **Think** **Write**

MAIN IDEA AND DETAILS

Write two places a person might find sprouts.

_____

_____

You can buy different kinds of sprouts at a store. Some are mild. Others are spicy. They taste different because they are grown from different kinds of seeds.

alfalfa sprouts

mung bean sprouts

radish sprouts

Stop | **Think** | **Write**

COMPARE AND CONTRAST

How are the alfalfa sprouts like the mung bean sprouts? How are they different?

_____

_____

Lots of seeds and some types of **grain** can be grown into sprouts. For example, radish seeds, broccoli seeds, and grains of wheat make **tasty** sprouts.

What is a detail about growing sprouts on this page?

_____

_____

Perhaps the best thing about sprouts is how easy they are to grow. You can grow them at home.

Stop **Think** **Write**

Why does the author point out that growing sprouts is easy?

_____

_____

All you need is a cup and some seeds.
Put the seeds in the cup, and add water.
Soak them overnight.

Stop | **Think** | **Write**

TEXT AND GRAPHIC FEATURES

Look at the photograph. What can you learn
about sprouts from this picture?

_____

_____

248

In the morning, pour off the water. Rinse the seeds twice a day. They will be ready in three to seven days. Sprouts offer good **nutrition**.

Stop | **Think** | **Write**

SEQUENCE OF EVENTS

To grow sprouts, what should you do after you soak the seeds overnight?

_____

_____

249

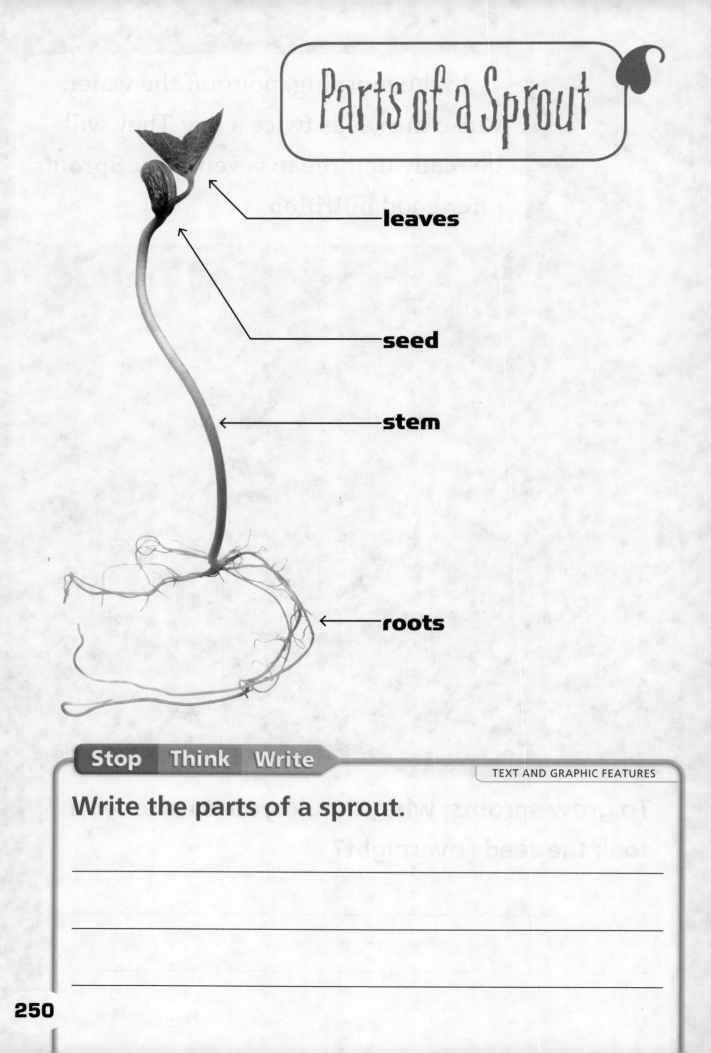

Parts of a Sprout

leaves

seed

stem

roots

TEXT AND GRAPHIC FEATURES

Write the parts of a sprout.

_____

_____

_____

1 **What do you need to grow sprouts?**

Hint

For clues, see pages 246 and 248.

_____

_____

_____

2 **How long does it take to grow sprouts?**

Hint

For a clue, see page 249.

_____

_____

_____

3 **Why is it a good idea to grow sprouts?**

Hint

For clues, look on pages 246, 247, and 249.

_____

_____

_____

Be a Reading Detective!

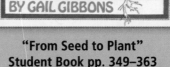

"From Seed to Plant"
Student Book pp. 349–363

Look back at "From Seed to Plant."

Think about the questions. Look for clues.

1 **What** does a plant need in order to grow?

2 **How** does a flower get pollinated?

Write your answer. Use details and examples from the selection.

1 **What** does a plant need in order to grow?

_____

_____

_____

_____

_____

_____

Talk about question 2. Tell about the clues you found.

2 **How** does a flower get pollinated?

✓ **TARGET VOCABULARY**

confused

ordinary

sensible

training

What a Teacher Does

1 A teacher is not an **ordinary** person. It takes a special person to teach!

What do you do after school on an ordinary day?

_____

_____

_____

2 Teachers need to know a lot. People need **training** before they can teach.

Name someone else who needs training.

_____

_____

_____

3 Teachers are **sensible**. They know when to work and when to play. They know how to solve problems.

Is it <u>sensible</u> to go out in the rain without an umbrella? Explain.

_____

_____

_____

4 When a child is **confused**, a teacher can help.

Tell about a time you felt <u>confused</u>.

_____

_____

_____

Mr. Reed's Last Day

by Claire Daniel

Today is Mr. Reed's last day. He is leaving his job. Mr. Reed is going back to school. He will be **training**. He will learn to teach computer skills to kids.

Stop Think Write

At his new school, Mr. Reed will be

_____ to be a better teacher.

It is his last day. His students know. They smile a lot. No one says a thing.

Mr. Reed wants to go learn more. It is a **sensible** thing to do. Still, he is not so happy. He is leaving. He thinks the children do not care.

Stop **Think** **Write**

UNDERSTANDING CHARACTERS

Why isn't Mr. Reed happy?

_____

_____

_____

The principal comes to class. She brings Curt and Gina. They wink at each other.

"Now I need Ann," the principal says. "Her father is here."

"This is odd," Mr. Reed says. The children just smile.

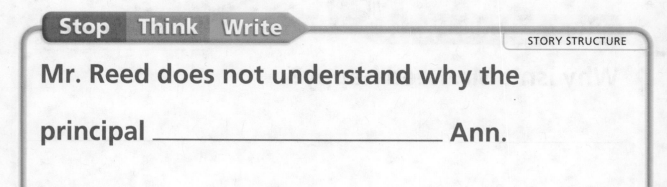

Stop Think Write

STORY STRUCTURE

Mr. Reed does not understand why the

principal _____ **Ann.**

All day long, the principal picks up children. Then she brings them back.

Mr. Reed gives the children a test. They do not mind. They smile and smile. Mr. Reed says, "That's odd, too."

Stop **Think** **Write**

STORY STRUCTURE

The principal picks up children and

_____ **them back.**

Then the principal asks for Ann, Gina, and Curt again. Now Mr. Reed is very **confused**.

Curt, Ann, and Gina come back. They have food, party hats, and a big box. "Surprise!" the children yell.

Stop | **Think** | **Write**

VOCABULARY

Mr. Reed is _____ because so many children come and go.

Ann says, "My dad brought this balloon."

Gina says, "The principal helped us write notes."

Curt says, "We put the notes onto the balloon. They will make you think of us."

Stop **Think** **Write**

STORY STRUCTURE

All the children wrote _____
as a surprise for Mr. Reed.

Now Mr. Reed is happy. He says, "This is no **ordinary** surprise!"

He ties the balloon to his bike. He rides home. The students wave. They will miss him.

Stop **Think** **Write**

STORY STRUCTURE

The surprise shows Mr. Reed that the children

will _____ him.

Look Back and Respond

1 What is the problem in this story?

Hint

For a clue, see page 255.

_____

_____

_____

2 What do the children do on Mr. Reed's last day?

Hint

For clues, see pages 258, 259, and 260.

_____

_____

_____

3 How does this story end?

Hint

For a clue, see page 260.

_____

_____

_____

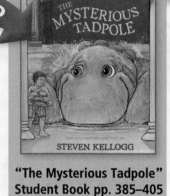

"The Mysterious Tadpole"
Student Book pp. 385–405

Be a Reading Detective!

Look back at "The Mysterious Tadpole."

Think about the questions. Look for clues.

1 **How** does Louis get money to build the swimming pool?

2 **What** makes Alphonse a special tadpole?

Write your answer. Use details and examples from the story.

1 **How** does Louis get money to build the swimming pool?

_____

_____

_____

_____

Talk about question 2. Tell about the clues you found.

2 **What** makes Alphonse a special tadpole?

✓ **TARGET VOCABULARY**

amazed

discovered

exact

remove

Different Kinds of Places

1 A boy dug in his yard. He had to

_____ some

rocks.

2 The boy _____

a tin box. It looked old.

3 A letter was in the box. He saw the date. It was long ago. Its

_____ date was

June 6, 1901.

4 The boy looked at the name. His great-grandma wrote the letter! The boy was

_____ !

Write the vocabulary word that best completes the synonym web.

5

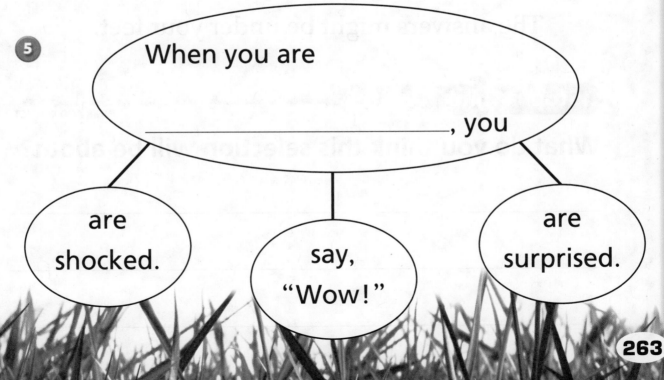

When you are

_____, you

are shocked.

say, "Wow!"

are surprised.

Discovering the Past

by John Berry

What was life like long ago? What did houses look like? What games did kids play? What did they eat?

The answers might be under your feet.

Stop | **Think** | **Write**

INFER AND PREDICT

What do you think this selection will be about?

_____

_____

_____

264

Things were left in the dirt. Time passed. Then people **discovered** the things. People found old coins. They found toys. They found old tools.

These old things are clues. They tell us about the past.

Stop Think Write

MAIN IDEA AND DETAILS

Old things can tell us about _____.

Some people study the past. It's a fun job. They dig in the dirt.

They find old coins. They find pots. They find tools. These things tell a story. It's a story of the past.

Stop   Think   Write

FACT AND OPINION

The author says that studying the past is a fun job. Is that a fact or an opinion?

_____

_____

_____

The diggers make a map. The map shows the **exact** places where people find things.

A coin may be deep in the dirt. The map shows where. A pot may be next to a wall. The map shows where.

Stop **Think** **Write**

VOCABULARY

The map is correct. It shows the

_____ place where people found things.

Scientists **remove** dirt. They study each item. They think about where it was found.

A toy was deep in the dirt. Another toy was near the top. The diggers may think the first toy is older.

Stop Think Write

Scientists clean the things that they find.

They _____ the dirt.

People learn from what they find. They thought a pot was for water. It looked like a water pot.

Then they looked closer. They found oil inside the pot. They found bits of food. They were **amazed**. The pot was for cooking!

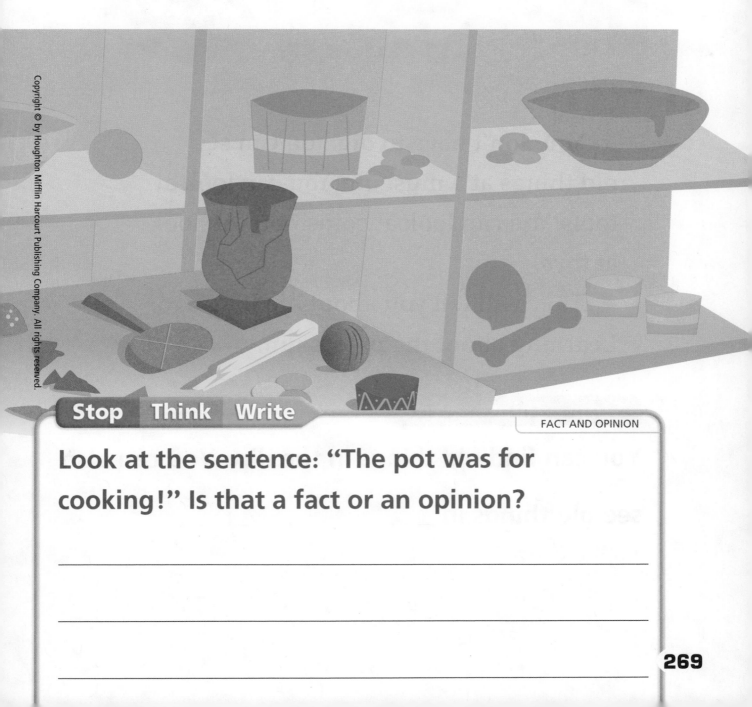

Stop **Think** **Write**

FACT AND OPINION

Look at the sentence: "The pot was for cooking!" Is that a fact or an opinion?

_____

_____

_____

You don't have to dig. You can see old things at a museum. You can look at tools. You can look at coins. You can look at toys.

They will tell you about life long ago. Learning about the past is fun.

Stop   Think   Write

MAIN IDEA AND DETAILS

You can find old things in the dirt. You can also see old things in _____.

Look Back and Respond

1 Which sentence on page 270 is an opinion?

Hint
Remember that you can agree or disagree with an opinion.

_____

_____

_____

2 Sometimes scientists change their minds about old things. Why?

Hint
For a clue, see page 269.

_____

_____

_____

3 Do you think digging for old things would be a fun job? Explain.

Hint
Think about what diggers do and what they discover.

_____

_____

_____

Be a Reading Detective!

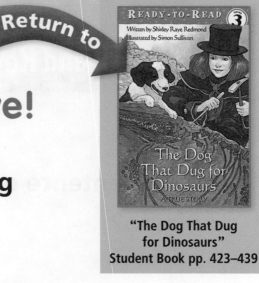

Return to

READY-TO-READ 3
Written by Shirley Raye Redmond
Illustrated by Simon Sullivan

The Dog That Dug for Dinosaurs
A TRUE STORY

"The Dog That Dug
for Dinosaurs"
Student Book pp. 423–439

Look back at "The Dog That Dug for Dinosaurs."

Think about the questions. Look for clues.

1 **What** are fossils?

2 **How** did Tray help Mary?

Write your answer. Use details and examples from the selection.

1 **What** are fossils?

_____

_____

_____

_____

_____

Talk about question 2. Tell about the clues you found.

2 **How** did Tray help Mary?

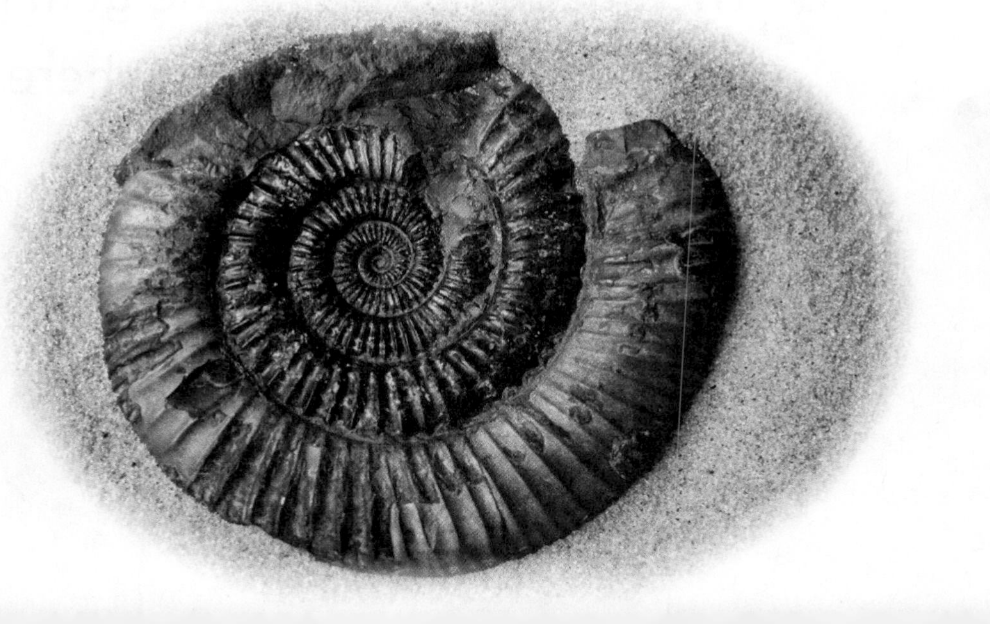

concealed

overjoyed

task

valuable

Once Upon a Time

Check the answer.

1. Will the prince be a good king? The queen wants to find out. She gives him a _____ to do. This job is not easy!

   ☐ **concealed** ☐ **task** ☐ **song**

2. The prince has to hunt for a _____ ring. It is made of gold and gems.

   ☐ **valuable** ☐ **silk** ☐ **overjoyed**

3. The queen has _____ the gem in a hiding place. It is somewhere in the woods.

   ☐ **concealed** ☐ **overjoyed**
   ☐ **lifted**

4 Tell about a time when you felt <u>overjoyed</u>.

_____

_____

_____

5 Name a <u>task</u> that you do at home.

_____

_____

_____

The Twelve Months

Based on a Czech fairy tale

adapted by Judy Rosenbaum

Marta lived with her stepsister, Vanda, and her stepmother. Marta was not treated well at all. She did all the housework. Vanda never had to do anything.

One December day, Vanda said, "I want strawberries. Go out and get me some!"

Marta didn't know what to do. Nothing grew in winter! Still, she went to look in the woods. She carried some bread for her lunch.

Stop | Think | Write

How do Vanda's words show what she is like?

_____

_____

_____

Snow was on the ground. The trees were bare. Marta walked and walked. Then she came to a campfire. Twelve people sat around it.

Marta greeted the people politely. They bowed to her. They made a place for her by their warm fire. This is how people treated travelers long ago.

Stop **Think** **Write**

MAKE CONNECTIONS

How many people were around the campfire? What else do you know that has this number?

_____

_____

Marta shared her bread with the strangers. The oldest man asked why she was in the woods. She explained her **task**.

The oldest man said, "June, help her." A woman pointed at the ground. Right away, a strawberry plant sprouted up through the snow. Soon, it had ripe, red berries.

Now Marta knew these people were not ordinary. They were the Twelve Months! The oldest man was December. The woman who made the strawberries grow was the month of June.

Stop **Think** **Write**

CAUSE AND EFFECT

What helps Marta see that the people are the Twelve Months?

_____

_____

Marta was **overjoyed**. She picked the berries. "Thank you!" she said.

Vanda met Marta at the door of their home. She grabbed the berries and ate them all. Then the questions started. "Where did you get these? Who gave them to you? Why didn't you bring more?"

Marta did not tell Vanda about the Months. She just said, "The berries were growing in the woods."

Stop | **Think** | **Write**

MAIN IDEA AND DETAILS

Who is asking all the questions? How do you know?

_____

_____

The next day, Marta's stepmother said, "I want roses."

Marta got ready to go. After she had left, Vanda said, "Mama, I don't trust Marta. I'm sure she has **concealed** something out in the woods. I think she has hidden something **valuable**, and I want it! I'll look for the flowers myself."

Vanda put on her warm coat. She carried a basket of food for herself.

Stop | **Think** | **Write**

VOCABULARY

If Marta has _____ something, she has put it in a hiding place.

It was easy to follow Marta's tracks in the snow. Soon Vanda saw the twelve people around the campfire. She didn't see any strawberries growing. So she didn't think she had reached the right place.

"Hello, traveler. What are you doing out on this cold day?" asked one of the men. Vanda didn't know it, but he was September.

"None of your business," Vanda said rudely. Then she walked away. She didn't share any of her food.

Stop **Think** **Write**

SEQUENCE OF EVENTS

What does Vanda see after she follows the tracks?

_____

_____

_____

December raised his hand. Heavy snow began to fall. It took Vanda hours to get home. Of course, she never found any roses.

A week later, Marta left the house for good. She went away to find a better life. She left two things behind. One was a note saying goodbye. The other was a bunch of roses.

Stop Think Write

MAKE INFERENCES

Where do you think the roses came from at the end of the story?

_____

_____

Look Back and Respond

1 **What is the first thing that Marta must find in the woods?**

Hint

For clues, see page 274.

_____

_____

_____

2 **What different things do June and December cause to happen?**

Hint

For clues, see pages 276 and 280.

_____

_____

_____

3 **What does December think of Vanda? How do you know?**

Hint

For clues, see pages 279 and 280.

_____

_____

Be a Reading Detective!

Return to

"Yeh-Shen"
Student Book pp. 457–465

Yeh-Shen
by Gina Sabella
illustrated by Jill Dubin

Look back at "Yeh-Shen."

Think about the questions.
Look for clues.

1 **What** is Yeh-Shen's problem at the beginning of the story?

2 **How** does the old man help Yeh-Shen?

281A

Write your answer. Use details and examples from the story.

1 **What** is Yeh-Shen's problem at the beginning of the story?

_____

_____

_____

_____

_____

Talk about question 2. Tell about the clues you found.

2 **How** does the old man help Yeh-Shen?

281B

grateful

odd

search

startled

Cats

Cats are silent when they walk. They can sneak up on you. You might be **startled** when you see a cat.

Cats are happy when you pet them. They purr to show that they are **grateful**.

This is an **odd** fact. A cat meows to people. It doesn't make that sound to other animals.

You can find out more about cats. You can **search** the library for cat books.

1 Cats are _____ when you pet them.

2 You can _____ for books in the library.

3 It's an _____ fact that cats don't meow to other animals.

4 Tell about one time when you were <u>startled</u>. What happened?

_____

_____

_____

Fluff, Gus, and Bob

by Richard Stull

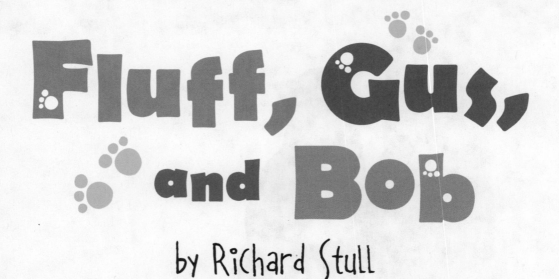

Fluff, Gus, and Bob lived together in a house. Fluff was an orange cat. Gus was gray. Bob was black and white.

Stop | **Think** | **Write**

STORY STRUCTURE

The orange cat's name is _____.

"Let's **search** the cupboard," said Fluff. "We'll find something to eat there." Fluff ran to the cupboard. She found cans of cat food.

"We can't open the cans," said Gus and Bob.

Stop | **Think** | **Write**

VOCABULARY

Fluff wants to _____ in the cupboard for something to eat.

"I know what to do," said Fluff. "Let's ask Jimmy to help."

"Jimmy doesn't know we can talk," said Gus and Bob. "He might find it **odd** that cats can talk."

UNDERSTANDING CHARACTERS

Which cat seems to make most decisions?

_____

_____

Just then, Jimmy came home from school. First he petted the cats. Then he turned on the TV to watch cartoons.

Fluff, Gus, and Bob all spoke at once. "Hey, Jimmy," they said. "We want something to eat."

Stop | **Think** | **Write**

SEQUENCE OF EVENTS

What is the first thing Jimmy does when he gets home from school?

_____

_____

287

_____

Jimmy jumped up from his chair. "Who said that?" he asked.

"We did," said the cats. "We're sorry if we **startled** you."

"You see, we're hungry," said Fluff.

"We're starving," said Gus and Bob.

Stop Think Write

CAUSE AND EFFECT

Why is Jimmy surprised?

_____

_____

_____

"Cats can't talk!" said Jimmy.

"Of course we can talk," said Fluff.

"Do you think we just sleep all day?" asked Gus and Bob.

"Well," said Jimmy. "Now I know that you can talk."

Stop **Think** **Write**

UNDERSTANDING CHARACTERS

Which two cats always talk at the same time?

_____

_____

_____

289

"I'm glad you can talk," said Jimmy. "I've got three new friends."

"Three hungry friends," said the cats.

"Oh," said Jimmy. "I almost forgot." He opened a can of cat food for his **grateful** friends.

Stop Think Write

VOCABULARY

The cats are _____ for the food.

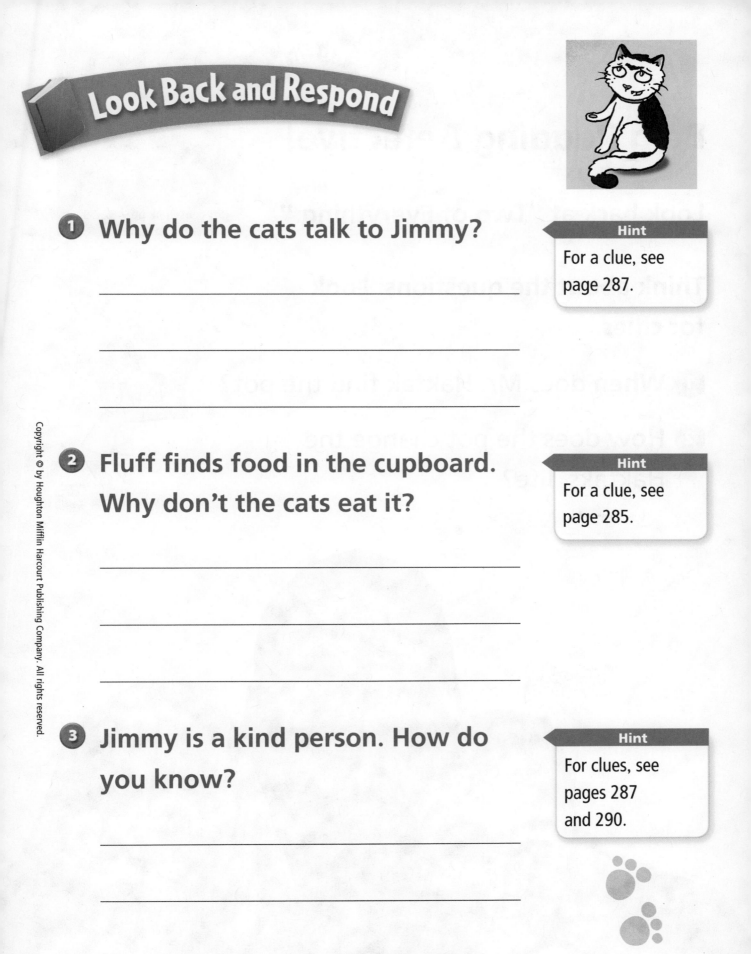

Look Back and Respond

1 Why do the cats talk to Jimmy?

Hint
For a clue, see page 287.

_____

_____

_____

2 Fluff finds food in the cupboard. Why don't the cats eat it?

Hint
For a clue, see page 285.

_____

_____

_____

3 Jimmy is a kind person. How do you know?

Hint
For clues, see pages 287 and 290.

_____

_____

_____

 Return to

 Two of Everything

"Two of Everything"
Student Book pp. 487–503

Be a Reading Detective!

Look back at "Two of Everything."

Think about the questions. Look for clues.

1 **When** does Mr. Haktak find the pot?

2 **How** does the pot change the Haktaks' life?

Write your answer. Use details and examples from the story.

1 **When** does Mr. Haktak find the pot?

_____

_____

_____

_____

_____

Talk about question 2. Tell about the clues you found.

2 **How** does the pot change the Haktaks' life?

A Farm Invention

1 Eli Whitney **designed** the cotton gin. It cleaned seeds from cotton.

Name something that was designed a long time ago.

_____

_____

_____

2 Whitney worked hard. His first plans were not good. At last he made a plan that worked. He was able to **achieve** his goal.

What do you want to achieve?

_____

_____

_____

292

3 The cotton gin was a **remarkable** machine. It helped people work faster.

Name a <u>remarkable</u> machine in your house.

_____

_____

_____

4 Farmers liked the cotton gin. They needed fewer workers. The **result** was cheaper cotton.

What might be the <u>result</u> of studying hard for a test?

_____

_____

_____

Cyrus McCormick and His Reaper

by John Berry

A Boy Who Made Things

Cyrus McCormick was born in 1809. He lived on a farm. He liked to make things.

Cyrus had a dream. He wanted to be an inventor. He made a new tool when he was fifteen. He used it to carry grain.

Stop **Think** **Write**

UNDERSTANDING CHARACTERS

Cyrus dreamed of being an

_____.

A Good Idea

Farmers cut grain by hand. They used a big blade. It was hard work.

Cyrus's dad wanted to cut grain faster. He **designed** a machine. He made it. It never ran right.

Stop | **Think** | **Write**

MAIN IDEAS AND DETAILS

Farmers worked many hours to cut grain. Cyrus's dad wanted to make the work

_____ .

Cyrus's Reaper

Cyrus wanted to try. He made a new machine. It cut grain fast. It would help farmers cut more. It was called a reaper.

He worked on the machine for ten years. He wanted to make it better. He wanted to **achieve** his goal.

| Stop | Think | Write |

MAIN IDEAS AND DETAILS

Cyrus wanted to make the reaper better. He worked on it for _____ years.

At last, Cyrus got a good **result**. The reaper worked better. It had an extra blade. It could cut grain in the rain.

Another man made a reaper. He wanted to have a contest. Whose reaper would work best?

Stop **Think** **Write**

The _____ of Cyrus's hard work was a better reaper.

Battle of the Reapers

The day of the contest was rainy. The other reaper jammed. Cyrus's reaper did not. It cut a lot of grain.

People wanted to buy Cyrus's reaper. He sold twenty-nine machines that year.

Stop **Think** **Write**

CONCLUSIONS

Cyrus was the _____ of the contest. His machine worked the best.

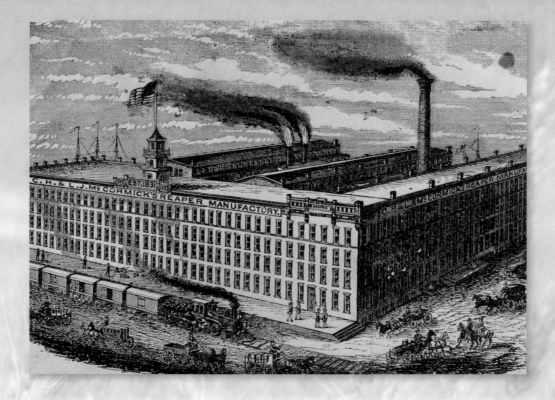

A New Place to Work

Cyrus made reapers on his farm. Many farmers wanted them. Cyrus needed more space.

He moved to Chicago. Workers in his factory made reapers fast. Cyrus sold thousands of machines each year.

Stop | **Think** | **Write**

COMPARE AND CONTRAST

Cyrus made more reapers at his

_____ than on his farm.

Success

The reaper was a success. Cyrus was famous all over the world.

He went to London in 1851. He got a medal for his work. His **remarkable** machine changed farming forever.

Stop **Think** **Write**

VOCABULARY

People thought the reaper was

_____.

Look Back and Respond

1 How did Cyrus's reaper change farm work?

Hint

For clues, see pages 296 and 297.

_____

_____

_____

2 How did Cyrus improve his machine?

Hint

For a clue, see page 297.

_____

_____

_____

3 Why did Cyrus move his work to a factory?

Hint

For a clue, see page 299.

_____

_____

_____

Return to

"Now & Ben"
Student Book pp. 521–539

Be a Reading Detective!

Look back at "Now & Ben."

Think about the questions. Look for clues.

1 **What** did Ben Franklin invent?

2 **Why** was Ben Franklin important?

Write your answer. Use details and examples from the selection.

1 **What** did Ben Franklin invent?

_____

_____

_____

_____

_____

_____

Talk about question 2. Tell about the clues you found.

2 **Why** was Ben Franklin important?

Summarize Strategy

You can **summarize** what you read.

- Tell important ideas in your own words.

- Tell ideas in an order that makes sense.

- Keep the meaning of the text.

- Use only a few sentences.

Analyze/Evaluate Strategy

You can **analyze** and **evaluate** a text. Think carefully about what you read. Form an opinion about it.

1. Think about the text and the author.
   - What are the important facts and ideas?
   - What does the author want you to know?

2. Decide what is important. Then form an opinion.
   - How do you feel about what you read?
   - Do you agree with the author's ideas?

Infer/Predict Strategy

Use clues to figure out what the author does not tell you. Then you are making an **inference**.

Use clues to figure out what will happen next. Then you are making a **prediction**.

Monitor/Clarify Strategy

Monitor what you read. Make sure it makes sense.

Find a way to understand what does not.

• Reread.

• Read ahead.

• Ask questions.

Question Strategy

Ask yourself **questions** as you read.

Look for answers.

Some questions to ask:

- What does the author mean?

- Who or what is this about?

- Why did this happen?

- What is the main idea?

Visualize Strategy

You can **visualize**.

- Make pictures in your mind as you read.

- Use words in the text to help you.

- Make pictures of people, places, things, and actions.

PHOTO CREDITS